How to

Self-Publish a Children's Picture Book

The Easy and Inexpensive Way to Create a Book and eBook

2nd ed.

For Non-Designers

INTERNATIONAL BOOK AWARDS FINALIST
IntlBookAwards.com

Eve Heidi Bine-Stock

Special thanks to:

Jill Arnel, editor, for her skill, tact, and generous spirit;

Hannah Kim, children's book illustrator, for cheerfully
providing artwork for color tests; and

Jean Batzell Fitzgerald, artist, for her unfailing encouragement.

Copyright © 2018 Eve Heidi Bine-Stock
ISBN 978-0-9831499-8-9

Cover illustration © helen_f, Fotolia
Beagle illustration © Jean Batzell Fitzgerald

Published by:

Eve Heidi Bine-Stock
P.O. Box 3346
Omaha, NE 68103

Contents

Introduction to 2nd Edition

Thank you to everyone who purchased the first edition of this work, and a special thank-you to those of you who contacted me by email to share your self-publishing experiences.

This second edition addresses the most common question that readers had: "How do I publish a book that has illustrations spanning two pages?" There is an easy way to do this, and this volume gives step-by-step help to accomplish it.

Since the publication of the first edition, Amazon has made a major change in the self-publishing landscape: they have merged their CreateSpace print-on-demand company with their KDP (Kindle Direct Publishing) arm.

Now, users can self-publish both print books and ebooks from one (KDP) dashboard. This second edition reflects the resulting changes in the publishing process.

If you have any questions, or just want to give me feedback, I invite you to contact me at:

EveHeidiWrites@gmail.com

I will answer your questions and address your comments by email and use them to improve this book for its next edition.

Kind regards.

Eve Heidi Bine-Stock
Omaha, Nebraska
August, 2018

Introduction to 1st Edition

You've finished your manuscript. Congratulations!

Now you've decided to publish your own book. Welcome to the world of indie publishing!

The word count is no more than 500-600 words. You've applied the concepts discussed in my three-volume series, *How to Write a Children's Picture Book*. You've received feedback from your critique group, from your children's writing instructor, and from an editor. The manuscript has been polished and proofread.

This book will provide you with all the information you'll need to self-publish a professional-quality printed children's picture book—even if you are not a graphic designer.

You'll learn how to publish your book with a print-on-demand (POD) company. Print-on-demand means that a copy of your book is printed only when someone orders.

No longer do you have to print 1,000 to 5,000 copies of your book at one time, with the enormous cost this entails. And you no longer have the cost of warehousing the books, and arranging for distribution.

Instead, the POD company deducts a printing charge (as each copy is printed) from your wholesale book price. Then they pay you the difference, so you *never* have to pay up-front to have a book printed. Another benefit is that the POD company ships the book directly to the customer. And that is one less thing to worry about!

You'll learn about the two major POD companies, Kindle Direct Publishing (KDP, owned by Amazon), and IngramSpark (owned by Ingram, the world's largest book distributor).

I'll take you step-by-step through the process of

- planning your book

- finding and working with an illustrator

- choosing fonts

- using Canva, an easy-to-use and inexpensive online design tool, to make the interior and cover of your book

- setting up an account and title with your POD company

- submitting book files to your POD company

- and, as a bonus, creating an ebook for free to sell on Amazon.com.

This book assumes that you have Windows 7 or newer, and an Internet connection.

If you have any questions, or just want to give me feedback, I invite you to contact me at:

EveHeidiWrites@gmail.com

I will answer your questions and address your comments by email and use them to improve this book for its next edition.

Kind regards.

Eve Heidi Bine-Stock
Omaha, Nebraska
November, 2016

Chapter 1
Planning Your Book: Cost and Price

The two major print-on-demand companies for indie publishers are KDP (an Amazon company which has replaced CreateSpace), and IngramSpark (a division of Ingram, the world's largest book distributor).

Quality options

Both KDP and IngramSpark print perfect-bound (with a spine) paperbacks.

IngramSpark offers three quality options for full-color books:

- Standard 50 lb. paper

- Standard 70 lb. paper

- Premium color on 70 lb paper.

The two Standard qualities are printed on industrial inkjet printers; Premium quality is printed on industrial laser printers and is substantially more expensive.

KDP has one quality option available for full-color books: 60 lb. paper. They don't disclose the type of printers they use.

IngramSpark's cover stock is heavier (thicker) than KDP's.

So let's compare KDP's 60 lb. paper with IngramSpark's Standard 70 lb.

Color Comparison

Before we compare price, here are a few words about the difference in color quality between IngramSpark and KDP.

KDP colors are more saturated (more intense), brighter and cheerier than IngramSpark colors. However, KDP colors are not very true to the colors in the original illustrations.

IngramSpark colors are less saturated, more muted, but they're truer to the original illustrations.

Both show a color shift, especially with blue shades. This is common; there's always a difference between how colors look on a computer monitor and how they look when printed because monitors and printers use different color systems.

TIP: If you're publishing a series, use the same POD company for all books in the series, so the colors are consistent.

Price Comparison

For the sake of comparison, let's assume that you are publishing a 32-page color book, the industry standard for a children's picture book, and are selling the book on Amazon.com for $9.97.

For a 32-page Color Book Selling on Amazon.com for $9.97		
Feature	**KDP**	**IngramSpark**
ISBN*	Free	$85
Barcode	Free	Free
Title setup	Free	$49 or Free
Revised file	Free	$25
Paper stock	60 lb.	70 lb.
Wholesale discount	40%	30%
Print charge	$3.65 all trim sizes	$2.13 small trim size** $2.78 large trim size**
Profit per copy sold	$2.33 all trim sizes	$4.85 small trim size $4.20 large trim size

*   International Standard Book Number. An ISBN uniquely identifies your book.
** Small: 4 x 6 to 6.14 x 9.21; large: 6.625 x 10.250 to 8.5 x 11

NOTE: To learn how to get your first title setup for free, see below in this chapter.

Bookstores and libraries

The above table shows a book being sold on Amazon.com. But what if you want your book to be sold by bookstores and libraries? The truth is, most of us are not such well-known writers that our books get into bookstores and libraries. So what's an author to do?

Conventional bookstores will not order your book from KDP, but they *will* order it from IngramSpark (or Ingram via Baker & Taylor for libraries).

Therefore, if selling your books to stores and libraries is your goal, plan on using IngramSpark and giving the usual wholesale discount, 55%. This allows the distributor to make some money, and bookstores and libraries will get their expected 40% discount.

So how much money will you earn on each copy sold to bookstores and libraries through IngramSpark at a retail price of $9.97? $2.36 for a small trim size, and $1.71 for a large trim size.

But keep in mind that bookstores demand the option to return books. In the past, they would order books and if the books didn't sell fast enough, they would send them back, causing you to lose money.

These days, booksellers tend to use "just-in-time" ordering practices. They order no more than they expect to sell and reorder when needed. So you can expect fewer returns.

IngramSpark does not allow you to set one discount for Amazon.com (and other online retailers), and a different discount for brick-and-mortar bookstores and libraries.

This means that if you set a 55% discount so bookstores and libraries can afford to order your books, you automatically set the same discount for Amazon.com (and other online retailers), and your profits will be low there, too. You'll make only $2.36 for a small trim size, and $1.71 for a large trim size, for online sales.

But there's good news! It's more lucrative to forego bookstore and library sales altogether and set up your title with IngramSpark at a 30% discount, sell your books on Amazon.com (and other online retailers), and make almost double the profit on each copy sold than if you were to use KDP.

On the other hand, using KDP has its advantages. Their ISBN, setup and revisions are free, so you'll need to sell fewer copies to recoup your expenses.

In any event, you will surely make more per copy by self-publishing than by receiving royalties from a traditional publishing house.

TIP: If you do book signings at a bookstore or library, you can order books directly from your POD company, have them shipped to yourself or to the signing location, and give the merchant or library their usual 40% discount. This still allows you to make good money.

Just be sure *to order your book at least three weeks in advance of your scheduled appearance.*

Distribution

When you publish a printed book through IngramSpark, they will make it available to *all* of their "distribution partners," which includes conventional bookstores and libraries, as well as online retailers such as Amazon, Barnes and Noble, Books-a-Million, and others. And, once you set your discount, you'll make the same royalty no matter where your book is sold.

Publishing a book through KDP effectively limits distribution to Amazon.com and Amazon UK and Europe because bookstores and libraries will not order from KDP.

KDP does offer "expanded distribution" to other online retailers, conventional bookstores, and libraries. But since bookstores and libraries won't order from KDP, that essentially limits "expanded distribution" to non-Amazon online retailers.

But there are two potential issues with "expanded distribution."

1) You're limited to what KDP calls "Industry Standard Trim Sizes" (see the next chapter for trim sizes); and

2) KDP requires a 60% discount for "expanded distribution," leaving you only pennies in royalties for each copy sold.

For these reasons, the "expanded distribution" option KDP offers is not such a great deal, after all.

Some self-publishers recommend that you distribute your books through KDP and IngramSpark simultaneously, in order to maximize your distribution options.

As I have not done this, I cannot advise you. However, should you wish to pursue this approach, simply Google the phrase "using both CreateSpace and IngramSpark" or "using both KDP and IngramSpark." You will find many reputable articles available to guide you.

Setting your retail price

For my comparison, I set the retail price at $9.97. Of course, you can set any retail price you want, as long as you make money. You *do* want to make money, right?

Since IngramSpark allows you to earn more per copy sold than KDP, if you publish through IngramSpark, you can set a lower retail price, and be competitive with traditional publishing houses.

You can always change your retail price if it is not selling well at your original price. Both KDP and IngramSpark have royalty calculators that will show you how much you'll make for any given retail price. (The next section will show you how to access and use their respective calculators.)

KDP lets you change the price at any time, and it will go into effect within about 48 hours.

IngramSpark updates retail prices only once a month, usually at the beginning of the month. Their site provides these precise dates when you use it to change your price. Their deadline for entering your new price is about a week before the update goes into effect.

NOTE: Since you may want to change your retail price at some point, do *not* have IngramSpark put the price in the barcode that appears on your book's back cover. That's why their default setting for "Price in barcode?" is "No." Otherwise, each time you decide to change the retail price, you must submit a new cover file, and *that* costs time and money.

KDP never puts the price in the barcode, so you don't have to worry about it.

Royalty calculators

You can access royalty calculators for both KDP and IngramSpark without even creating an account first, or logging in.

Here's how to access and use the calculators:

KDP

1. Go to kdp.amazon.com.

2. If you are not logged in, click "Learn how easy it is." If you *are* logged in, under "Create a New Title," click "See all Getting Started tips."

3. On the left side of the screen, a list of "Help Topics" appears.

4. Click the "Royalties" link.

5. Scroll down and click on the "Paperback Royalty" link.

6. Click "How we calculate paperback royalties."

7. This screen has an explanation, as well as a Royalty calculator which you can download to your computer. It's easy to use!

IngramSpark

1. Go to www.IngramSpark.com.

2. Click the Resources tab.

3. Click Tools.

4. Scroll down to "Publisher compensation calculator" and click.

5. Provide the requested information. Here are some useful tips:

- ISBN is optional, so you can leave this blank.

- Interior Color and Paper – Choose Color, then Standard 70.

- Binding Type – Choose Paperback, then Perfect Bound.

- Laminate Type – Choose Gloss.

- Duplex Cover – Choose No.

6. When you've provided all the necessary information, click Calculate.

The result will be displayed.

Why you would want to buy ISBNs on your own

We've already seen that IngramSpark charges $85 for an ISBN, which is a discount off the regular price of $125 for a single ISBN; and it's your own ISBN, not IngramSpark's. This means that your imprint name (your "brand name") is listed as the publisher, not IngramSpark. Since there are thousands of publishing houses and imprints, no one will know that your book is self-published, and is more likely to judge it on its merits.

If you plan to self-publish more than one book with IngramSpark, you can save a lot of money if you buy a block of ten ISBNs directly from the ISBN agency at www.ISBN.org for $295. That's less than $30 each! A bargain if you plan to publish several books during your writing career. (Don't buy the barcode; IngramSpark will provide that for free.)

What about KDP? While it is true that they will give you a free ISBN and barcode, KDP will be listed as the publisher. So people will know that your book is self-published, and may have second thoughts about buying it.

If you opt to buy your own block of ten ISBNs from the ISBN agency, KDP will allow you to use them. Then your imprint name will be listed as the publisher.

KDP does provide the opportunity to purchase your own ISBN from the ISBN agency at the discounted price of $99 (instead of the regular price of $125), but this option is not an integral part of the book setup workflow.

The easiest way to access this option is from your KDP Bookshelf. Under "Create a New Title," click the "More about ISBNs" link.

On the page that appears next, click "Paperbacks." Then click the link, "Can I provide my own ISBN?" Next, click "buy an ISBN at a discounted price." This will take you to the ISBN agency to purchase a single ISBN for $99.

Whew! Maybe someday, Amazon will provide an easier way!

No matter which ISBN option you choose, KDP will provide a free barcode.

How to set up a title for free with IngramSpark

IngramSpark charges $49 to set up a title. Google **IngramSpark coupon** and you may find a code or button for a free setup of your first title. (Just be sure to get the coupon code, or click the discount button *before* you sign up with IngramSpark.)

Here's another way to get a free title setup: If you place a single order for 50 or more copies of your book within 60 days of setup, IngramSpark will credit you the $49 setup fee. This offer applies to all titles you set up with IngramSpark—not just to your first title.

Now you know how much printing and distributing your own book will cost and how much you'll make, so let's plan your book's layout.

Chapter 2
Planning Your Book: Layout

Before you contact an illustrator, determine the layout of your book. You need to know the dimensions of your book and its layout. Then you can tell your illustrator what dimensions you need for the images and the number of images you need.

As a publisher, you have more things to consider than when you were "just" a writer.

Some of the things you need to consider are:

- Number of pages.

- Where to put the copyright page.

- The text on each page.

- "Page-turner" text on odd-numbered pages.

- Page size.

- Font size.

- Illustration size(s).

1. What counts as a "page"?

A single sheet of paper has two pages, one on the front (also called the "recto") and one on the back ("verso").

The first page of the book is page number 1. Whether or not a page number actually appears is irrelevant. The back of that sheet of paper is page number 2. It appears on the left-hand side of your book. And the facing page on the right-hand side is page number 3.

This means that every right-hand page will be an odd number (1, 3, 5, etc.), and every left-hand page will be an even number (2, 4, 6, etc.).

2. How many pages should my book have?

The industry standard is 32 pages for a children's picture book. This includes the title and copyright pages.

IngramSpark lets you print a perfect-bound (paperback with spine) color book between 17 and 899 pages long. They will add 1 or 2 pages for their control code to make the total page count an even number.

KDP has a minimum of 24 pages and requires you to submit an even number of pages. They will add 2 pages for their control code.

3. Where should I put the copyright page?

You have the choice of putting your copyright page at the front or the back of your book.

If you place it at the front of your book, on page 2 (which is the back of the title page), your story would start on page 3 (the right-hand page). In this case, you would have both an illustration and text on page 3.

If you put the copyright page at the back of your book, you would start your story on page 2 (the left-hand page). In this case, you could have an illustration on page 2, and text on the facing page, which is page 3. Setting "page-turner" text on an odd-numbered page encourages readers to turn the page!

One advantage to putting the copyright page at the back is that it does not draw attention to the fact that your book is self-published. The reader encounters just the title page and then the beginning of your story.

When readers use Amazon's "Look Inside" the book feature, you draw them into your book right away without wasting their time on a copyright page. This increases your chance of engaging their interest and making a sale.

If your story allows it, put your copyright page at the back of the book. This way, you can have an illustration on an even-numbered page and the text on the facing odd-numbered page—which is the "page-turner."

4. Should I have a dedication page?

You really don't need a separate dedication page. You can put your dedication at the top of the copyright page, in a font that is larger than the rest of the text on the page. You could choose one that matches your title or name font. This will look very attractive.

5. Make a first draft book dummy

Take a printout of your manuscript.

Add the title page and, possibly, the copyright page, before your story begins. (Just write notes on the printout.)

Break down the printout to determine what text will go on each page. This gives an idea of the actions or scenes that will be depicted in the accompanying illustrations.

Use a pencil (and eraser!) to indicate the breaks on the printout. Write the page number next to the text that goes on each page.

Then take eight pieces of 8.5 x 11 inch paper (letter size). Hold them together horizontally, and fold them in half vertically. You will have 32 pages, the typical number of pages for a children's picture book. Write the page number at the bottom of each page. Do this even if the page number will not appear in the final book.

Now take your printout, and cut your manuscript where you have written break marks with your pencil.

Tape the strips of paper onto the pages of your dummy, taking care to place page-turner text on odd-numbered pages.

As with a recipe, "adjust according to taste." This means that you may need to change the text that goes on each page until it's just right.

6. What size should my book be?

The head children's librarian at the New York Public Library says that the most popular trim size for a children's picture book is 8" wide x 10" high.

She was quick to point out, though, that picture books come in many different sizes.

She cautions against very small trim sizes because they tend to get lost among larger books. She also discourages very large trim sizes because they're difficult to carry home in a bag or tote. An 8.5" x 11" trim size— offered by both KDP and IngramSpark—works great!

The children's book buyer at Barnes & Noble corporate headquarters in New York confirmed that they buy children's picture books in virtually any size—as long as it is less than 12" wide and less than 12" high.

Keep in mind that 6" x 9" is most commonly used for trade paperbacks— fiction or nonfiction— and not for children's picture books.

Always consider the cost of printing, and the discount you offer. (Review Chapter 1, "Planning Your Book: Cost and Price," once you've determined which size works for your book.)

7. Trim sizes for KDP and IngramSpark

The trim sizes in the table below are for perfect-bound paperback (with a spine), color books. Dimensions are page width x length in inches. For KDP, "E" indicates "Expanded distribution;" "C," Custom size. For IngramSpark, "P" indicates "Premium color."

Trim Size	KDP	IngramSpark
Small		
4 x 6		+
4 x 7		+
4.25 x 7		+
5 x 7		+
5 x 8		+
5.5 x 8.25		+
5.5 x 8.5	E	+
5.83 x 8.27 A5		+
6.5 x 6.5		+
6 x 9	E	+
6.14 x 9.21	E	+

Trim Size	KDP	IngramSpark
Large		
6.625 x 10.250		+
6.69 x 9.61		+
7 x 10	E	+
7.5 x 9.25		+
8 x 8		+
8 x 10	E	+
8 x 10.88		+
8.25 x 6 landscape	C	
8.25 x 8.25	C	
8.25 x 10.75		+
8.25 x 11		+
8.268 x 11.693 A4		+
8.5 x 8.5	E	+
8.5 x 9		+
8.5 x 11	E	+
11 x 8.5 landscape		P

Note that IngramSpark has one size that is wider than it is tall (called "landscape" orientation), which is 11" x 8.5". This size is only available in the more expensive "Premium color." (To determine your cost and profit for this, use the Publisher Compensation Calculator discussed in Chapter 1.)

KDP, on the other hand, has a landscape trim size that is 8.25" wide x 6" high. KDP also offers "Enter My Own Trim Size" for color books, so you can make other trim sizes:

Min. trim width	4"
Max. trim width	8.5"
Min. trim height	6"
Max. trim height	11"

8. What size should the illustrations be?

First, let's discuss the interior of your book. Then we'll "cover the cover."

a. Interior illustrations

Determine what size the illustrations should be after you first decide between two options:

i.   The pictures inside your book are smaller than the page size, with a white margin all around

ii.   The pictures inside your book run to the very edge of the page.

Let's discuss these options separately.

i. Pictures smaller than page size

For interior pages having pictures that are smaller than the page size, allow a page margin of one-half (0.5) inch.

This means that the illustrations would be one inch shorter and one inch narrower than your page dimensions. So, for example, a book with a trim size of 8" x 10" would have illustrations that are 7" x 9".

ii. Pictures run to edge of page

For pictures that run to the edge of the page, it's best to think in terms of a three-step process:

a.   First, ask the illustrator to create pictures with the width being the same as the trim size, and the height being the trim size *plus* 0.125" on the top and bottom, or trim size+0.25". For example, for an 8" x 10" trim size, the picture would be 8" x 10.25".

b. For an illustration that spans two pages, the starting width would be double-wide, for example, 16" x 10.25", which your illustrator would then cut in half (using software), to create an 8" x 10.25" image for the left-hand page, and another 8" x 10.25" image for the right-hand page. (Rather than actually cutting the image in half, your illustrator can copy one half of it and save it as a new image, and do the same thing for the other half.)

c. Third, ask the illustrator to use software to "expand the canvas" of a half-illustration by adding a 0.125" white strip on the bind side only. This will give you a half-illustration+white strip that is, for example, 8.125" x 10.25" in total.

(The even-numbered page will have the white strip on the right side; the odd-numbered page will have the white strip on the left.)

For illustrations that span two pages, that white strip on the bind side will ensure that the two halves of the illustration "line up" without losing any of the illustration in the gutter.

Adding that 0.125" white strip will also shift the illustration, so that it extends past the trim line on the side opposite the bind side. This portion (called the "bleed") will be trimmed off during the manufacturing process, and your final picture in your finished book will extend to the edge of the page.

Similarly, for the height, 0.125" will be trimmed off both the top and bottom, and the final result will be a picture that extends to the edge of the page at the top and bottom.

To sum up, for a trim size of 8" x 10", make your *page* size 8.125" x 10.25", and make your *picture* size 8" + 0.125 white strip on bind side (or 8.125" total width) x 10.25".

iii. For both options

Make all of your illustrations for the book interior the same size. This is easier to request from your illustrator, and easier for you to work with later when you use a design tool to lay out the pages of your book. (That'll all come later.)

Remember that you need an illustration for your title page. You'd be surprised how many people forget!

b. Cover illustrations

Let's talk about the illustrations for your front and back covers.

Often you can re-use an illustration (or a portion of one) that appears inside the book and place it on the cover.

After the illustrator has given you the images for the inside of the book, you can decide whether you need additional illustrations for the front and back covers. But it's helpful to let the illustrator know up-front that you may need the additional illustrations.

If you decide you *do* want additional illustrations, ask your illustrator to provide them in a size equal to your book's interior illustrations.

9. Make a second draft book dummy

Use a word processing program such as Microsoft Word.

To determine the page size and the width of the margins, consider which option to choose for the illustrations:

a) The pictures inside your book are smaller than the page size, with a white margin all around

b) The pictures inside your book run to the very edge of the page.

a. Pictures smaller than page size

For interior pages having pictures that are smaller than the page size, set your page size so it's the same as the trim size. For example, for a trim size of 8" x 10", set the page size to 8" x 10".

Margins

Set all margins to one-half (0.5) inch.

b. Pictures run to edge of page

If you want pictures to run to the edge of the page, make the page size larger than the final trim size of your book.

For the width of the page, add 0.125" to the trim size. For the height of the page, add 0.25" to the trim size. (What you're really doing is adding 0.125" to all sides *except* the bind side.)

For example, for an 8 x 10 trim size, your page size would be 8.125 x 10.25.

Margins

The margin should be 0.625" on all sides of the page except for the bind side. The margin on the bind side should be 0.5".

To set up these margins, follow these steps using Microsoft Word:

1. Go to the Page Layout menu and choose "Margins."

2. From the drop-down menu, click "Custom Margins...."

3. A window will pop up, called "Page Setup":

4. In the middle of the window it says, "Multiple pages." From the drop-down menu, choose "Mirror margins."

5. Now look near the top of the window, where it says "Margins." For Top, Bottom and Outside, enter 0.625. For Inside, enter 0.5. Then click OK.

Your margins are now set correctly for the text in a book having pictures that run to the edge of the page.

c. For both options

Copy and paste the text from your manuscript onto the appropriate page. (Don't retype the text; this will only introduce errors.)

Do not justify the right margin. Leave it ragged or center your text.

Use a font size approximate to the one you intend to use for the final, printed book, which will probably be around 18 point. Your font size will be limited by the size you need to fit the longest text you have on a single page.

For your copyright page, 10- or 11-point font is a good size to use. (In a later section, you'll learn what to place on your copyright page.)

Add the page number to the bottom of each page, even if it won't appear in your final book. This will help you keep track of where you are as you work.

For pages with illustrations, type "illustration size" and the dimensions of the needed illustration. For example, for an 8" x 10" trim size book having pictures smaller than the page size, you would type:

Illustration size: 7" x 9"

For pages having an illustration that runs to the edge of the page, and using the same example trim size, you would type:

Illustration size:
Width: 8" for picture + 0.125 white strip on bind side
Height: 10.25" for picture

NOTE: You will need to show this book dummy to your illustrator.

TIP: When viewing your pages on your computer screen, look at them individually since, in a two-page spread view, Microsoft Word doesn't display the pages correctly. The left- and right-hand pages are displayed backwards! (Perhaps Microsoft has corrected this in the latest version of Word.)

Print out your dummy. Tape individual sheets of paper together back-to-back as needed, so they combine to make two pages, one on the front and the other on the back.

Voila! You have your second draft book dummy. Count the number of illustrations.

You have determined the size(s) of your illustrations and how many illustrations you need. Next up is finding an illustrator to work with...

Chapter 3
Finding and Working with an Illustrator

You have determined the size and approximate number of images you need for your picture book. Now is the time to find an illustrator.

This section covers:

1. Where to find an illustrator.

2. Working with your illustrator.

3. Re-naming files you receive from your illustrator.

1. Where to find an illustrator

Two of the best places to look for children's picture book illustrators are www.UpWork.com and www.Guru.com.

Both allow you to search for "children's book illustrator," which, for some reason, gives more affordable results than "children's book *illustration.*"

Both show portfolios of artwork.

Both give the illustrator's name, location, ratings and comments from clients, and hourly rates. You can also negotiate a flat fee per illustration or for the whole project. A flat fee arrangement benefits you, the client, more because you know in advance how much you'll pay.

If you pay your illustrator an hourly rate, Guru and UpWork track the time spent online working and takes screen shots of the illustrator while she works. This ensures that you pay only for the actual hours worked.

When you find an affordable illustrator whose work you like, you can contact her for a quote through Guru's or UpWork's Website.

Both Guru and UpWork let you post a job and have illustrators submit proposals with bids for the work. You can then view their ratings and portfolios to choose someone whose work you admire.

Wait a day or two after posting a job to allow illustrators to reply from different time zones around the world.

Be sure to negotiate with the illustrator ahead of time regarding the number of revisions that will be included in the price.

How much can you expect to pay? Many excellent illustrators in countries such as Turkey, Romania, and India charge $10 to $15 an hour. Again, you can also negotiate an affordable flat fee per illustration or for the entire project.

One children's book writer I know hired an illustrator on Guru and the illustrator charged $9 per picture—and the pictures were beautiful and professional. Apparently, 9 U.S. Dollars is a lot of money in the illustrator's country.

Both UpWork and Guru help you establish deadlines and milestones, and provide payment protection for you and for the illustrator.

You pay UpWork (by credit/debit card or PayPal) or Guru (by PayPal, credit/debit card or e-check), and they hold the payment in escrow. They only pay illustrators when they meet deadlines and milestones.

UpWork charges an additional 2.75% processing fee for payments, while Guru doesn't. In fact, Guru gives you 3.5% cash back for paying by e-check, bank account, or wire transfer.

Both UpWork and Guru provide dispute resolution.

You may have heard of Fiverr as an affordable Website for finding illustrators, but the artwork on UpWork and Guru is more professional and varied in style.

Also, Fiverr is known for its "up-selling." For example, an illustrator might charge $5 for a black and white drawing of half a figure (say, lying in bed); $10 for a color image of half a figure; $20 for a color image of a whole figure; an additional $20 for a background scene; add $20 for each additional whole figure.... By the time you're done, you're paying $40 to $100 for each illustration!

The illustrators' terms on UpWork and Guru are more straight-forward.

Fiverr also pesters you with numerous emails after you sign up. UpWork and Guru don't.

No matter which Website you use, illustrators often charge more for cover art than they do for page illustrations.

SCBWI

I'd be remiss if I did not discuss finding an illustrator who is a member of the Society of Children's Book Writers and Illustrators (www.SCBWI.org).

You do *not* need to be an SCBWI member yourself to look for illustrators on their site.

Many fine members of the SCBWI have not yet illustrated a book and are eager prove themselves and enhance their portfolios. The SCBWI Website has links to illustrator Websites with portfolios. Check out these portfolios to find styles that work for you.

You are likely to pay more for an illustrator who's an SCBWI member since most members live in English-speaking countries where the cost of living is higher.

She may also require royalties in addition to a flat fee. If you offer her a percentage of the net profits, tell her how much she would be making per copy.

Email an illustrator whose style you like. Explain that you are a member of the SCBWI (if you are) and that you are publishing your own children's picture book. Give her any publishing credits and reviews you may have. Explain to her that you admire her work and would like her to create X number of illustrations.

Ask her what her fee is per illustration. Ask her what she'd charge for the whole project. Ask her how many revisions are included in the fee. Try to negotiate at least two.

She will probably want you to pay half the fee up-front and then additional sums when various milestones are reached.

When working with an SCBWI illustrator, it's best to have at least a letter signed by both of you, spelling out the terms of your working relationship.

You would, at the very least, state the working title of your book, number of illustrations she will create for you, dimensions of the illustrations, and the fee per illustration or whole project.

If you will also pay her a percentage of your net profits for each copy sold, or a percentage of the retail price for each copy sold (both are a type of royalty), include this in your letter. Add that you will pay her whenever the royalties amount to $10. You can pay by PayPal.

Include the milestones and number of revisions in your letter.

Also, in writing, set a deadline for completion, from the date of signing the agreement.

Agree to credit her as the illustrator on the book's cover, and in the information you provide through your distributor to booksellers and libraries.

Include your name, address, phone number and email address for both yourself (the "Publisher") and for your illustrator.

Work with your illustrator on drafts of your letter until you both agree on all the terms.

You may find it worthwhile to refer to the legal guides for authors and self-publishers, written (separately) by Helen Sedwick and Tad Crawford.

The final step is for both of you to initial the bottom of each page, and sign and date the letter. The easiest and fastest way to do this is electronically, by using the free online service offered by www.HelloSign.com. It's a breeze!

Once the letter has been signed by both of you, be sure to download it from HelloSign to your computer and keep it for your records. Remember to forward a copy to your illustrator!

2. Working with your illustrator

After you've hired your illustrator, email her the "second draft book dummy" (see Chapter 2, "Planning Your Book: Layout"), since it shows which text goes with each illustration and its size.

Confirm with her the exact size(s) of the illustrations you need.

Ask your illustrator to email you the final artwork files as "AdobeRGB (1998), 300 ppi, 8 bits per channel, PNG non-interlaced, optimized palette."

- RGB is the color system used by your computer monitor. AdobeRGB (1998) has the widest available range of colors.

- Eight (8) bits per channel is the color depth and 300 ppi is the resolution your print-on-demand company needs.

- PNG is the file format.

If a file is too large (in Megabytes) to send by email, suggest that your illustrator use a free online service such as Hightail (at www.Hightail.com).

Trust your illustrator's imagination to determine how the pictures will appear. Many talented illustrators have come up with much better ideas than I ever could!

Ask your illustrator to send you sketches and finished illustrations as she creates them. Then, you can efficiently provide her with constructive and effective feedback.

Later, you may determine that you need additional illustrations for the front and back covers of your picture book. In this case, negotiate the price for this as another, separate job, through Guru, UpWork, or your SCBWI illustrator.

3. Re-naming files you receive from your illustrator

You will probably need to rename the original illustration files you receive from your illustrator.

Start with whatever name the illustrator gives it. Then, at the beginning of the filename, add the page number (for example, "2-") that the illustration goes on.

Finally, at the end of the filename, add "-orig" (for original) to the file name.

Keep this original file unchanged and in a safe place, so you can always refer back to it if necessary.

Now that you're all set with an illustrator, it's time to choose a font for your story and your copyright page.

Chapter 4
Choosing a Font for Your Story and Copyright Page

Once you receive the first completed illustration for your book, choose the font for your story and copyright page.

Selecting a font can be fun and creative. Choose with an eye to making it compatible with the style of the illustrations and the theme of your story.

TIP: Now is the perfect time to get feedback from your critique group or from other people whose opinion you trust.

This chapter covers:

1. Two basic kinds of fonts.

2. Which font to use for your story.

3. Which font to use for your copyright page.

4. How to download and install a font.

5. What needs to go on the copyright page.

6. How to update your book dummy.

Let's get started!

1. Two basic kinds of fonts

Fonts come in two kinds: *serif* and *sans serif*.

Look at the letters F W S and T. The little short lines coming off the upper and lower ends of these letters are called "serifs."

The font you are reading now is a serif font.

"Sans serif" means, literally, "without serif."

Trebuchet (the font you are now reading) is a sans serif font.

See the difference?

IMPORTANT: Always use a serif font for the text inside your children's picture book. Serif fonts are much easier to read in a book.

2. Which font to use for your story

In this section, I've included fonts available on Canva.com, the easy, inexpensive online design tool you'll use to create your book. Since many of these are original *and* attractive, using one of them will give your book a distinctive, professional look.

Obtain most of these free fonts from www.fontsquirrel.com (except where indicated). I'm showing them to you in a size you're likely to use for a children's picture book (18 point, except where indicated).

IMPORTANT: Whatever you do, avoid using "Times New Roman." Choosing this font will instantly mark you as an amateur!

So, without further delay, here are my suggestions for fonts to use for your story:

Aleo The quick brown fox jumps over the la

Alike 1001fonts The quick brown fox jumps

Arvo The quick brown fox jumps over th

Droid Serif The quick brown fox jumps ov

Libre Baskerville 16 point The quick brown

Lora The quick brown fox jumps over the l

Lustria 1001freefonts.com The quick brow

Luthier befonts.com The quick brown fox ju

Marta 1001fonts.com The quick brown fox ju

Merriweather 16 point The quick brown fox j

Old Standard The quick brown fox jumps over

Playfair Display The quick brown fox jumps

Prata 1001fonts.com 16 point The quick brown

PT Serif The quick brown fox jumps over the

Quattrocentro Roman The quick brown fox

Sanchez befonts.com The quick brown fo

Source Serif Pro The quick brown fox jumps

Trocchi 16 point The quick brown fox jumps o

Vidaloka The quick brown fox jumps over the laz

Vollkorn The quick brown fox jumps over the

Download and install fonts you like to your own computer (see section "4" below for how to do this). Then you can choose them from the font menu in Microsoft Word. You'll need to do this when you update your book dummy to show the size and layout of text.

If you download Sanchez, look in your "Downloads" folder for a filename that starts with "Latinotype."

3. Which font to use for your copyright page

For the copyright page, use the same font you chose for the story text. Use a small size, 10- or 11-point work well here.

If you have dedications on your copyright page, put them in the same font as the title or as the names on your cover, but in a larger size than the rest of the copyright page text. Chapter 6, "Choosing Fonts for Your Cover and Title Page," will show you the way.

4. How to download and install a font

When you click the "download" button or link on a font Website, the font will automatically download to your computer's "Downloads" folder.

To install the font, follow these steps:

a) Open your "Downloads" folder.

b) Select (highlight) the font folder and double-click.

   If "Extract all files" appears above the workspace, click on it to un-zip the folder.

c) Select the font file and double-click. On the small window that pops up, click Install.

NOTE: If the font folder you've selected has bold (bd) or italic (it) fonts in addition to a regular one, install only the regular font. Also, if there is both a TTF (True Type Font) and OTF (Open Type Font), download *only* the TTF.

5. What needs to go on the copyright page

Even if you don't have all the information you need to complete your copyright page yet, it's a good idea to fill in as much information now as you can. Be sure to update this page before you use Canva to create the copyright page for the final book.

At the top, put:

Dedications, if any, from author and illustrator, in a larger font than the rest of the copyright page. Limit each dedication to one line (with a blank line between them), and use initials only to indicate the author and illustrator. It will look something like this:

To loving mothers everywhere.–J.B.

For my mom.–L.S.

Then drop down at least two lines. In the same font you use for your story (but in a smaller size, like 10- or 11-point), use this template to fill in your information:

[Title of book]
Text copyright © [year of publication] [author name]
Illustrations copyright © [year of publication] [illustrator name]
ISBN: [XXX-X-XXXXXXX-X-X]

Drop down two lines. Then put:

NOTE: Yes, that's "express," and not "expressed."

Drop down two lines. Then put:

Published by:

[your name or imprint name]
[physical address if you have a P.O. box
or use a mailbox service;
don't put your home address]
[Web address]
[your email address; put this only if
you don't have a physical or Web address]

TIP: I think it looks best if you center all the above information, as I did.

6. How to update your book dummy

After you choose the font you want, use Microsoft Word to edit your book dummy, to show the font in the size and layout it will appear in the final book. This will be your third draft book dummy.

Compare your font sizes to those used in other children's picture books. Printing out a page of your book and holding it next to a book designed by a traditional publishing house works well for this purpose.

Use the same font size for all the pages of your story (but not for the title or the copyright pages). Never mix font sizes in your story unless you want to emphasize something in the text, such as:

closer

closer

closer

TIP: You can choose a font size that is different from those provided in Microsoft Word's drop-down menu. Just highlight the size field, type a number, and press Enter.

TIP: Your text will be more pleasing if you do the following:

1. Go to Paragraph settings.

2. Set "Spacing before" and "Spacing after" to zero (0).

3. Set "Line Spacing" to Multiple, At 1.4. This is the default line spacing in Canva, set by professional graphic designers.

NOTE: Microsoft Word is fine for making a book dummy, but you can't use it to create your actual book. Word isn't built for inserting illustrations that take a lot of memory and it will crash. The effort you put into your dummy *is* essential, as you will discover.

You've chosen the font for your story and copyright page, and updated your book dummy to show the font and proper layout. Now it's time to use Canva to create the interior of your book.

Chapter 5
Using Canva to Create
Your Book's Interior

Now that you know which font you will use for your story and copyright page, and have updated your book dummy to reflect this, you can begin creating your book in earnest!

You will be using Canva (www.Canva.com), an easy-to-use (but powerful) online design tool, to create the pages of your book.

TIP: To ensure that all Canva features work as expected, use the most recent version of Chrome or Firefox for your browser.

Canva is free for basic use, which is all you'll need to create your book's interior. Just sign up with your email address.

When it comes to designing your book cover, you'll need to upgrade to the advanced version, "Canva for Work," which costs only $12.95 a month, with the first month free. (See Chapter "8" for more details.)

Learn everything you need to know about Canva for your book's interior pages:

1. Canva "designs."

2. Getting started.

3. Renaming your design.

4. Making a placeholder title page.

5. Making a placeholder copyright page.

6. Creating pages with story text.

7. Creating pages with an illustration.

1. Canva "designs"

A "design" is Canva's term for a file. It can have text, pictures, and design elements such as shapes and lines.

A design can have as many as 30 pages, but since you'll be using illustrations that consume a lot of memory, you *do not* want your browser to freeze!

There's an easy way around this problem. Make three designs for your book's interior:

- one for pages 1-10

- a second one for pages 11-20

- a third one for pages 21-32.

I'll show you how to easily combine them.

2. Getting started

This is what Canva looks like after you've signed up:

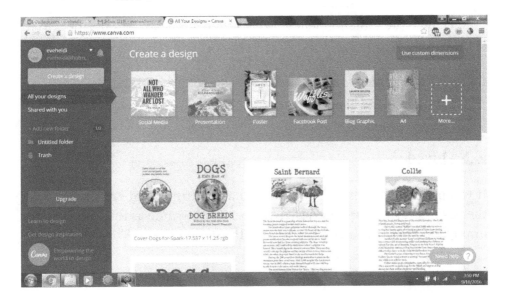

In the lower part of the screen, you can see designs I've already created. When you first sign up with Canva, you won't have any designs of your own there. Instead, there will be sample designs, like those in the upper part of the screen.

To create your first design, which will be for pages 1-10 of your book's interior, click "Use custom dimensions" in the upper-right corner:

The following feature will pop up:

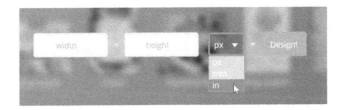

First change the units to inches. Then, enter the width and height of your book's interior.

Below is your guide for both "No bleed" and "Bleed" options.

a. No bleed

If you planned your book's interior to have pictures that are smaller than the page size, set your new design size so it's the same as the trim size. For example, for a trim size of 8" x 10", set the design size to 8" x 10".

b. Bleed

If you planned your book's interior to have pictures that run to the edge of the page, you must make the design size larger than the final trim size of your book.

For the width, add 0.125" to the trim size. For the height, add 0.25" to the trim size. (What you're really doing is adding 0.125" to all sides *except* the bind side.)

So, for example, for an 8 x 10 trim size, your design size would be 8.125 x 10.25.

c. For both options

After you enter the dimensions for your new design, click the "Design!" button.

3. Renaming your design

Right now, your design is untitled, but shows the dimensions:

To give your design a meaningful name, click the "untitled" name it has as a placeholder. The following window will pop up:

Give your design a name like "p 1-10 [book title] [design dimensions]."

Then click Done.

4. Making a placeholder title page

Page 1 of your new design will be the title page. We're not going to work on it now. That will come later when you create your cover.

For now, you can leave page 1 blank, or type "Title page" by following the steps in "6." below.

Then add a new page by clicking "Add a new page," located below your design page (as shown here):

5. Making a placeholder copyright page

If your copyright page is at the beginning of your book (on page 2), just leave it blank for now, or type "Copyright page" by following the steps in "6." below.

Then add a new page, which will be page 3.

Come back to the copyright page to finish it after you have created pages with story text.

6. Creating pages with story text

If you're familiar with the basic features of Microsoft Word, you'll be comfortable using Canva to create pages with story text because they share many of the same features.

Canva also provides an easy way to center a block of text on the page.

a. Activating the text function

On the left side of your screen, click T for Text:

Sample text will appear:

b. Selecting sample text

Click "Add subheading." A text box will appear on your design page, with sample text highlighted inside:

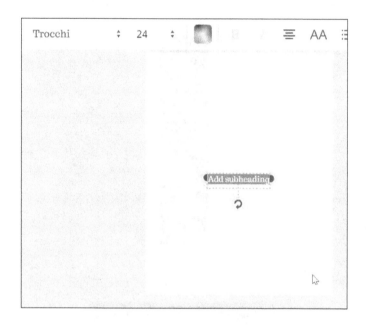

c. Selecting font and size

Choose your font from the Font drop-down menu (see below). This should be the same font you decided on earlier in Chapter 4, "Choosing a Font for Your Story and Copyright Page."

For size, choose the same font size you used in Microsoft Word:

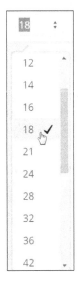

NOTE: You can use a size that is not on the menu by entering your desired size in the highlighted field above the menu, and pressing Enter.

d. Copying and pasting story text

By copying and pasting the text, you keep errors from creeping back in and even adding new ones that often appear when we retype the text.

Select the text from your book dummy in Microsoft Word and copy it by pressing Ctrl+c (that is, the Ctrl and c keys at the same time).

Go back to Canva. The sample text should already be highlighted. So just go ahead and paste your story text by pressing Ctrl+v. The sample text will be replaced by your story text:

e. Aligning text

The Canva default alignment is "centered." You can also choose to align your text to the left. However, right alignment is usually not used in a children's picture book.

To change the text alignment, simply click an icon from the menu below:

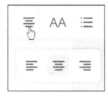

f. Centering the text box

Move the cursor under the text box until it turns into a four-headed arrow. Then double-click and drag the text box until you see dotted vertical and horizontal lines. These lines show that your text box is centered:

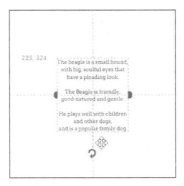

(**A note for sticklers for detail:** For a book designed with bleed, you added 0.125" to the trim size of the width. (For example, an 8" wide trim size was designed to be 8.125" wide with bleed.) Center the text horizontally the same way for no-bleed and bleed books because the difference between the two is negligible (half of 0.125" or only 0.0625" or 1/16"). No reader will even notice.)

Now that you know how to create pages with story text, you can finish your copyright page the same way. Just use a smaller font size, such as 10- or 11-point.

7. Creating pages with an illustration

Canva provides an easy way to work with illustrations:

a. Uploading an illustration

On the left side of your screen, click Uploads:

Then click "Upload your own images":

Now browse your computer for your desired illustration.

b. Putting an illustration on a design page

With your design page open, click the uploaded image you want to place on the page.

It will appear on the page, smaller than the design size, but not in its original size. We must—and will—resize the image to fit your planned book design.

c. Re-sizing the illustration

i. No bleed

As a reminder, "No bleed" means you planned your book's interior to have pictures that are smaller than the page size, with a 0.5" margin on each side.

You know the original width and height in inches of your illustrations. You must now convert inches to pixels. Just follow these steps:

1. Go to www.unitconversion.org. In the search box, enter **pixel.**

2. You'll get three options. Choose option "3. Typography: pixel (Y)."

3. Choose "inch" in the "From" list. Choose "pixel (Y)" in the "To" list.

4. Enter the width of your illustrations in inches; the width in pixels will appear. Make a note of this information. Then do the same for the height of your illustrations.

Now, return to Canva, where you placed your image on a design page.

To resize the image, use the double-headed arrow to drag the lower-right corner of the image until the numbers at the corner show the correct width and height in pixels. Bingo! *That's* the right size.

Click to end the resizing function, and you're done!

ii. Bleed

"Bleed" means you planned your book's interior to have pictures that run to the edge of the page after the book is trimmed.

Right now, your image looks smaller than your design page. You need to fit the image to the design page. It's a snap:

Press the Ctrl and Alt and "f" keys at the same time.

And you're finished!

d. Centering the illustration

This section applies only to "No bleed" books.

Move the image until the vertical and horizontal dotted lines show a centered image:

Notice that you have a 0.5" margin on all four sides, just as you planned.

e. Adding text over an illustration

For adding text over an illustration, see "6.a" through "6.e" above. (You don't need "6.f" because you're not likely to center your story text over an illustration. You'll place the text where the illustration allows sufficient space for it.)

Next you'll learn how to change the text color.

f. Changing the color of text over an illustration

Traditional publishing houses tend to use only two colors for story text:

- black text over light-to-medium colors

- white text over red and dark colors.

These choices ensure your text will be easy to read over the illustration.

In Canva, the default color is black. To change the text to white, click the color wheel icon below:

The following window will pop up:

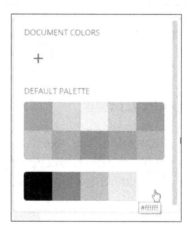

Click the white box indicated by "#ffffff." The text color will turn from black to white.

Congratulations! You've finished the interior of your book!

Later, when you learn how to create your cover, you'll also complete your title page.

Next, you'll choose fonts for your title page and cover.

Chapter 6
Choosing Fonts for Your Cover and Title Page

Choosing fonts for the cover and title page is a lot of fun!

There are a few criteria to consider when selecting an appropriate font for your book title. Some of them are:

- It must be easy to read.

- It must be large enough to read in the small thumbnail-sized image that appears on Amazon.

- It must complement the style of the illustrations.

- It must go well with your book's theme and content.

- It must be age-appropriate for your target audience.

This chapter answers these questions:

1. Which fonts will work best for your front cover and title page?

2. How many fonts can I use on the front cover?

3. What kinds of fonts look best together?

4. Which font should I use for the back cover?

5. Which font(s) should I use for the title page?

6. How do I download and install a font?

1. Which fonts will work best for your front cover and title page?

This section contains a wide variety of fonts I recommend for the title and names on the front cover and title page of children's picture books.

I have divided the list into sections: Serif, Sans Serif, Handwriting, Script, and Fancy.

I indicate which ones are available on Canva for free, as well as the Websites for downloading free fonts, whether or not they are already available on Canva.

The only fonts I show you here that you need to pay for cost only $5 apiece. They are from the talented designer, Kimberly Geswein, and are available from www.dafonts.com.

You can always upload a font you like to Canva if it is free for commercial use, or if you have paid for commercial use.

Experiment with different fonts using Microsoft Word before you begin creating your cover and title page with Canva.

If your book title is short, try all caps and see how you like it. Using all caps gives your title an entirely different look and feel which might be just right for your book. It's fun and useful to experiment.

TIP: Avoid *Comic Sans MS* or *Kristin ITC* or *Segoe Print.* These Microsoft Office fonts will instantly brand you an amateur.

Below is my list of recommended fonts by category:

Serif

Abril Fatface Canva fontsquirrel The quick

Alike 16 point Canva 1001fonts The quick brown f

Arvo 16 point Canva fontsquirrel The quick br

Benjamin Serif – ufonts The quick brown fox j

Berkshire Swash Canva 1001fonts The quick br

Coustard 16 point Canva 1001fonts The quick

Duality 1001fonts The quick brown fox jumps over th

Emily's Candy Canva 1001fonts The quick bro

Glass Antiqua Canva 1001fonts The quick brown fox j

Huxtable 1001fonts The quick brown fox jumps ove

Janda Curlygirl Chunky 14 point $5 dafonts Th

Janda Quirkygirl $5 dafonts The quick brown fox jumps

Maiden Orange 1001fonts The quick brown fox jumps over th

Merriweather 16 point Canva fontsquirrel Th

Minya Nouvelle 1001fonts The quick brown

Peralta 1001fonts The quick brown

Playfair Display Canva fontsquirrel The quic

Playfair Display Black Canva fontsquirrel

Purple Purse 1001fonts The quick brown fo

Quando 16 point Canva 1001fonts The qui

Ragg Mopp NF 1001fonts The quick brown f

Ribeye Canva 1001fonts The quick bro

Risque 1001fonts The quick brown fox jumps o

Rye Canva 1001freefonts The quick br

Sanchez Canva befonts The quick brown f

Spicy Rice 16 point 1001fonts The quick brown fox jum

SUNDAY 16 POINT CANVA BEFONTS THE QUICK B

Trocchi 16 point Canva fontsquirrel The quic

Sans serif

25 CENT COMICS 16 POINT UFONTS THE QUICK BROWN F

Amaranth Canva 1001fonts The quick brown fo

Archivo Black Canva 1001fonts The

Archivo Narrow Canva 1001fonts The quick brown fox

Arimo Canva 1001fonts The quick brown fox

Bubblegum Sans 1001fonts The quick brown fox jumps ov

Cantora One Canva 1001freefonts The quick bro

Carter One Canva 1001fonts The quick br

Chewy Canva 1001fonts The quick brown fox jumps

Coolvetica Rg 1001fonts The quick brown fox ju

CREEPSTER CANVA 1001FONTS THE QUICK BROWN FOX JU

crushed canva 1001fonts The quick Brown Fox Jumps ov

Fredoka One Canva 1001fonts The quick

Hammersmith One Canva 1001fonts The q

HURRY UP 1001FONTS THE QUICK BROWN FO

Jempol 1001fonts The quick brown fox jumps over the lazy d

KG Behind These Hazel Eyes $5 Dafonts Th

KG WHY YOU GOTTA BE SO MEAN $5 DAFONTS THE QUICK BRO

Kite One Canva 1001fonts The quick brown f

Kronika 16 point 1001fonts The quick brown

Lilita One Canva 1001fonts The quick brown fo

LUCKIEST GUY 1001FONTS 16 POINT THE QUICK BRO

MAIL RAY STUFF 1001FONTS THE QUICK BROWN FO

McLaren 1001fonts The quick brown fo

Montserrat Canva fontsquirrel The quick

Montserrat Light Canva fontsquirrel The

Mouse Memoirs 1001fonts The quick brown fox jumps over the lazy d

Nunito Canva 1001fonts The quick brown

Nunito-Light Canva 1001 fonts The quick br

Oregano Canva 1001fonts The quick brown fox jumps over t

Original Surfer 1001fonts The quick brown

Oswald Canva 1001 fonts The quick brown fox jump

Rum Raisin 1001fonts The quick brown fox jumps over th

Snickles 1001fonts The quick brown fox jumps over the lazy dog. The

Teen 1001fonts The quick brown fox jump

Handwriting

Abscissa 1001fonts The quick brown fox jumps ov

Airplanes in the Night Sky $5 dafonts The

Coming Soon Canva 1001fonts The quick bro

Crafty Girls Canva 1001fonts The quick

Elephant Hiccups 14 point $5 dafonts The quick

Gargle Rg 1001fonts The quick brown fox jump

Gochi Hand 20 point Canva 1001fonts The q

JANDA CAPSLOCK 16 POINT $5 DAFONTS THE

KG Life is Messy 14 POiNT $5 dafoNTS The quick bRO

KG Primary Italics 22 point $5 dafonts The

KG Primary Whimsy 22 point $5 dafonts The

Over the Rainbow Canva 1001fonts The quick

PERMANENT MARKER CANVA 1001FONTS THE

KG Piece by Piece $5 dafonts The quick brown fox ju

Schoolbell Canva 1001fonts The quick brown fox ju

Shadows Into Light Canva 1001fonts The quick bro

Script

5th Grade Cursive 12 point 1001fonts The quick brown

Allura 22 point Canva 1001fonts The quick bro

Clicker Script 20 point Canva 1001fonts The quick bro

Euphoria Script 20 point Canva 1001fonts The quick brow

Grand Hotel 20 point Canva 1001fonts The quick brown fo

Great Vibes 20 point Canva 1001fonts The quick brow

Janda Cheerful Script $5 dafonts The quick brown f

Janda Happy Day 14 point $5 dafonts The quick

Kaushan Script Canva fontsquirrel The quick bro

KG Always a Good Time 14 point $5 dafonts The quick b

Lobster Canva 1001fonts The quick brown fox jumps

Montez 20 point 1001fonts The quick brown fox jumps o

Niconne 20 point Canva 1001fonts The quick brown f

Oleo Script Canva 1001fonts The quick brown fox ju

Pacifico Canva 1001fonts The quick brown fox jum

Parisienne 20 point Canva 1001fonts The quic

Playlist Script Canva befonts The quick brown fox jump

Princess Sofia Canva 1001fonts The quick brown fox ju

Sacramento 24 point Canva 1001fonts

Satisfy Canva 1001fonts The quick brown fox jumps o

Yellowtail Canva 1001fonts The quick brown fox jumps over

Fancy

Janda Apple Cobbler Solid $5 dafonts The

KG Alphabet Regurgitation 15 point $5 dafonts The

KG Melonheadz 16 point $5 dafonts The quick brown fox

Pineapple Delight 15 point $5 dafonts The quick

2. How many fonts can I use on the front cover?

If the title font is very easy to read in a smaller size, you could also use it for the names. Here's an example using one font:

Title
Names

But that's boring, don't you think? How can we make this more appealing? Adding just one more font can do wonders. However, the maximum number of fonts you should plan on using on the front cover is two. One for the title and another for the names. The next section will provide you with guidelines and examples.

3. What kinds of fonts look best together?

Often, the font used for the title is different from the font used for the names of the author and the illustrator. This is particularly true when the title font is especially heavy or distinctive. In this case, it's a good idea to use a plain sans serif font for the names.

An example of a heavy font is **LUCKIEST GUY**. In this case, it would be best to use a plain sans serif font for the names, such as **Nunito**, **Archivo Black** or **Kronika**.

Here is an example of the title in a heavy or distinctive font, and the names in a simple, upper- and lowercase sans serif font:

Names

or this:

Title

Names

You could also set the title in all caps in one sans serif font and the names upper- and lowercase in the same sans serif font, like this:

TITLE

Names

or reverse, like this:

Title

NAMES

Another popular combination is an upper- and lowercase serif font for the title, and a simple, sans serif font in all caps for the names, like this:

Title

NAMES

or this:

Title

NAMES

Just make sure that any combination you use is easy to read, and pleasing to the eye. Get feedback from your critique group or anyone else whose opinion you trust.

4. Which font should I use for the back cover?

It's best to use a font on the back cover that you used on the front. This will give you a unified look.

Use a font that is very readable in upper- and lowercase when set in a small size.

If you used such a font on the front cover, use that one, too, for the back cover.

If you didn't, then you'll need to find a different font for the back. In this case, you can't go wrong if you use a simple, upper- and lowercase sans serif font.

If you used a script font or an uppercase font on your front cover, you can use that on the back cover as a heading, but not for a block of text.

It's very possible that if you have a large illustration on your back cover, you might not need any text at all!

TIP: For a block of text on your back cover, first type it in Microsoft Word, with a 0.625" margin. Make sure there are no typos, and then copy and paste the text onto the Canva design.

5. Which font(s) should I use for the title page?

For your title page, use the same font(s) you chose for your front cover.

6. How do I download and install a font?

When you click the "download" button or link on a font Website (such as www.1001fonts.com), the font will automatically download to your computer's "Downloads" folder.

To install the font, follow these steps:

a) Open your "Downloads" folder.

b) Select (highlight) the font folder and double-click.

   If "Extract all files" appears above the workspace, click on it to un-zip the folder.

c) Select the desired font file and double-click. On the small window that pops up, click Install.

NOTE: If the font folder you've selected has bold (bd) or italic (it) fonts in addition to a regular one, install only the regular font. Also, if there is both a TTF (True Type Font) and OTF (Open Type Font), download *only* the TTF.

TIP: If you download a font from ufonts.com, look in your "Downloads" folder for a filename that starts with "ufonts.com."

IMPORTANT: Do *not* delete the font from your "Downloads" folder; you *will* need to access it there later!

Now that you've selected your fonts, it's time to plan your cover and title page.

Chapter 7
Planning Your Book Cover
and Title Page

You have already used Canva to create "designs" for your story and copyright page. Before you use it again to create your front and back covers and your title page, you must consider some simple design principles and plan the "look" of your covers.

This is the fun and creative part of making your own book. And it's arguably the most important because people *do* tend to "judge a book by its cover."

This chapter will answer the following questions about design principles:

1. Where should I put my cover illustration and text?

2. How many colors can I use?

3. Which colors go well together?

4. What size(s) should I use for the cover text?

5. How do I indicate contributor roles?

6. Can I put a border around the edge of the cover?

7. What should I put on the back cover?

8. Can I base my title page on the front cover?

1. Where should I put my cover illustration and text?

There are two basic approaches to creating your cover:

a) Let's first look at the case where your illustration runs to the very edge of the cover after it is trimmed during processing.

   In this case, superimpose your title over the upper part of the illustration, and contributor names over the lower part.

   If your illustration has big stretches of background, place your title and names over them.

   If your illustration is very "busy" in the lower portion, raise the names to the middle or upper area of the cover, but under the title.

   You can either re-use an interior illustration for your cover that best represents your story, or ask your illustrator to create a new picture especially for the cover.

b) Now let's talk about where to put an illustration that does *not* run to the very edge of the cover. The illustration fits within the margins of the cover.

   Approach "b)" gives you at least the following options:

   i.   Re-use an entire interior illustration as-is, and superimpose the title and contributor names over it.

   ii.   Re-use an entire interior illustration and shrink it to make room for the title and contributor names. This is what *The Paper Bag Princess* does in the edition I have.

   iii. Use a portion of an illustration by cropping. When this is done, it is often the top part of the illustration that is cut off. This is what my edition of *The Napping House* does. The cropped illustration sits in the lower part of the cover because it's the "heaviest" object of the design.

iv.   Put a border around a portion of an illustration. The framed portion is usually placed on the cover where it allows room for the title above the framed portion, and contributor names below it.

Wherever you put the title and contributor names, the general rule is to put the title above the names. Here's the exception: If you are a famous author, on the order of a David Shannon or a Kevin Henkes, you can put your name above the title in a relatively large font.

2. How many colors can I use?

Aside from the colors in your illustration, the maximum number of colors you should use for other cover elements is three.

The background is color #1, the title is color #2, and the names are color #3. (You *don't have* to use three colors; the title and names can be the same color.)

White background? That's a color.

Black text? That's another color.

Border? That's a color, too. (If you have a border, try using the same color for your title and see how that looks.)

Take your cue from colors in the illustration and use them for other cover elements.

Remember, you *don't have* to use three colors; that's the maximum. Two could be plenty!

TIP: Traditionally, the background color of the back cover is the same as the one on the front.

3. Which colors go well together?

Here are some successful color combinations:

- White goes with everything. That includes white text on another-colored background.

- Orange and teal

- Blue and yellow

- Pink and purple

- Green and light blue

- Green and yellow

- Red and green

- Red and black

- Yellow, purple and red

Take your cue from the colors in the illustration, and use them for other cover elements, too. Your illustrator has surely used pleasing color combinations.

4. What size(s) should I use for the cover text?

Let's look at the different text elements separately. There is text for the title, for contributor names, and on the back cover.

Make important text larger, but avoid mixing font sizes on the same line of text.

If your title is on more than one line of text, make the less important text smaller like this:

PIGS
ON A
RAFT

or this:

The
Trouble
with
Teddy

Both examples look good—and professional. See how easy that was?

TIP: A good rule of thumb is to make the small text about half the size as the bigger text.

Here's an actual book title. Notice that "The" is on a separate line:

The
Paper Bag Princess

That's how the title appeared (with a different font) when the book was first published.

Note that "The" is not centered. And that's okay when you have one small word because it doesn't throw the title off-balance. It still looks professional and polished.

But you *don't* want to do this:

The
Paper Bag Princess
and the
Prince

Why not? Because it's not balanced. The left side is too heavy and looks like it will tilt down like a see-saw.

This actual book title is divided in half. This shows both halves as equally important:

The Princess
and the Pea

Now here it is again, with only the important words in a larger size:

The
Princess
and the
Pea

Which is better? There's no "right" answer. Both are balanced. Both are used by traditional publishers. Both have good reasons for their sizes and placement.

IMPORTANT: Do what works to enhance the importance of the words, the meaning of the story, and the visual balance.

NOTE: Use a larger font size for the title than the ones used in the examples above. The exact size you use depends on the specific font you choose, the length of your title, the size of your cover, and the size of your illustration. The important words in your title could be as tall as 72-point for a large-sized book.

TIP: Don't make your title so big that the cover looks crowded. Leave plenty of "blank" space.

Contributor Names

Make contributor names smaller than the title. As a guide, try a font size between 13- and 21-point for a large-sized book.

Back Cover

The font size for the back cover should be smaller than that used for the front. Try a font size between 13- and 21-point for a large-sized book.

5. How do I indicate contributor roles?

You have several options when it comes to indicating contributor roles. Here are the most common ones:

a) If you write

Written by

then match it with

Illustrated by

b) If you write

Story by

then match it with

Pictures by

or

Illustrations by

or

Art by

For "a" and "b" above, you can put the name next to, or under, the role.

If you put the name *next to* the role, then center them with the author above the illustrator, like this:

[role] by [author name]

[role] by [illustrator name]

If you put the name *under* the role, then put the author on the left and the illustrator on the right, like this:

[role] by	[role] by
[author name]	[illustrator name]

If you follow "b" above, you don't have to use the word "by" if you put the role *above* the name, like this:

[role]	[role]
[author name]	[illustrator name]

After all, words such as "Story," "Pictures," "Illustrations," and "Art" don't need a "by" with them if they're visually separated from the name.

c. You don't have to mention the role at all.

You could put just the author's name above the illustrator's name, like this:

[Author name]

[Illustrator name]

or put the author's name on the left and the illustrator's name on the right, like this:

84

[Author name]   [Illustrator name]

Traditional publishers all use the above options, so you can't go wrong whichever one you choose.

6. Can I put a border around the edge of the cover?

Don't plan on having a border around the cover at the very edge. This is because the POD company trims your cover in processing, and the borders will almost certainly turn out uneven and won't look good.

7. What should I put on the back cover?

You could have an illustration.

You could have text which describes your story.

Or both.

Just don't crowd your back cover.

Leave room on the back for the barcode, which your POD company will put on for you on the bottom right of your back cover.

For KDP, the barcode is 2" wide x 1.2" high.

For IngramSpark, it's 1.75" wide x 1" high.

Be sure the barcode area is at least 0.5" from the bottom and right side of your back cover.

I'll show you how to do this easily in Chapter 8, "Using Canva to Create Your Book Cover and Title Page."

8. Can I base my title page on the front cover?

Yes! The easiest way to make your title page is to copy elements you want to re-use from your cover and paste them onto your title page.

We'll go into this in more detail in the next chapter, when we create your actual cover and title page.

Chapter 8
Using Canva to Create
Your Book Cover and Title Page

You have already used Canva for free to create "designs" for your book's interior.

However, to create your book cover and title page, you must upgrade to the 30-day free trial of "Canva for Work." This should allow you sufficient time to complete your book. But if you need "Canva for Work" longer than 30 days, it costs only $12.95 a month, and you can cancel any time.

If you later sign up again for "Canva for Work" to create another book, all your designs and any uploaded fonts will be there, waiting for you.

This chapter covers the following topics:

1. Uploading fonts

2. Getting and using ColorZilla

3. Determining the spine width

4. Setting the front cover size

5. Placing an illustration on the front cover

6. Cropping an illustration

7. Putting a border around a cropped illustration

8. Creating text

9. Ensuring front cover elements fit within the "safety zone"

10. Creating your back cover

11. Assembling your cover

12. Creating your title page

13. Getting feedback.

TIP: That's a lot, I know. Take your time, and please read through the entire chapter before beginning to work.

1. Uploading Fonts

Now is the time to upload to Canva the fonts you selected for your cover and title page. This applies only to the ones Canva doesn't already have.

You can upload a maximum of 10 fonts before you must delete one to make room for another. If you delete any fonts that you used for your cover or title page, the deleted fonts will remain in your designs, so don't worry!

Before you upload a font, you need to prepare the font file. To do so, follow these steps:

a) Go to your computer's "Downloads" folder. If the font you want appears as a simple file (and is not in a folder), you don't have to do anything to the file. Read the next section, "Here's how to upload a font."

b) If the font you want is in a folder, you need to open the folder and find your font file.

c) Copy the font file by pressing the Ctrl and "c" keys at the same time.

d) Then go up a level (or two) to the "Downloads" folder again. Paste your font file there by pressing the Ctrl and "v" keys at the same time.

e) Your font file is now ready to upload to Canva.

Here's how to upload a font:

a) On the Canva homepage (the one with all your designs in the lower part of the screen), click "Your brand":

b) The following window will appear:

c) Scroll down until you see "Upload new font" (see below).

d) The "Open" window will appear. Browse your computer for the "Downloads" folder. Then select the desired font file.

e) After you select the font you want to upload, you'll be prompted to confirm that you have the right to use it:

You *do* have the right because the fonts I showed you are either available on Canva for free or available elsewhere and free for commercial use. Or perhaps you paid $5 to use one of Kimberly Geswein's fonts.

So click "Yes. Upload away!"

Success! You've just uploaded a font to Canva!

You'll notice that the font has been added to the top of the font menu:

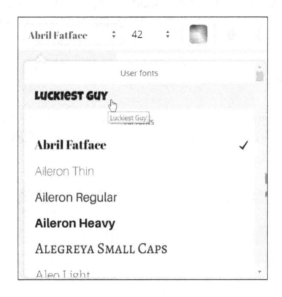

2. Getting and Using ColorZilla

ColorZilla is a color-picker that identifies the color code of an object or area in an illustration. You can then enter the code in Canva's color-wheel window and get the exact color you want.

This is useful when you want to change the background color of your cover to something that matches a color in your illustration.

Or you want the change the color of the title or contributor names from black to something else matching a color in your illustration.

Or you want to change the color of a border that you've place around a cropped illustration.

For example, you may see a red flower in a patch of grass, or a blue bandana on a yellow duck, and you want to use that shade of red or blue for the title or border.

Go to www.colorzilla.com to download the application. Then install it. It's small and takes no time at all. When installed, a little color-wheel icon will appear near the top-right side of your browser window.

Here's how to use ColorZilla:

a) With the design you're working on open, click the ColorZilla color-wheel icon at the top-right side of your browser window. Your screen will look like this:

b) Move the cross-hair cursor around your illustration until you see a color you like. The code for that color appears at the top of the small ColorZilla window, and starts with "#". Write down the code along with a description, such as "dark green."

Choose a few different colors, writing down the code and description for each. This way, you'll be able to try them out and see which one you like best.

c) When you are finished choosing colors, press the Esc key to end the ColorZilla function.

d) Now click the design element whose color you want to change.

e) If the design element is a background shape (which, in this example is black), or a border, Canva's "Pick a color" function will appear as a little colored square at the top of your Canva workspace:

If the design element you're working on is text, a little color-wheel icon will appear:

f) In either case, to activate Canva's "Pick a color" function, click the icon. The following window will appear:

g) Click the "+" button. The following window will appear:

h) Type the code (without the "#") of a color you like. The design element will change color. Try a few colors and see which one you like best.

If you want white, after all, the code is ffffff (that's six f's).

i) When you are satisfied, press Esc to end the color-picker function.

And that is how simple it is to use ColorZilla!

3. Determining the spine width

The spine width for KDP is determined by multiplying the number of pages by 0.002347". This means that for a 32-page color picture book, the spine width is 0.0751".

The spine width for IngramSpark does not have a simple formula. But there is a simple way to find out what it is. Just follow these steps:

a) Go to www.IngramSpark.com.

b) Click the Resources tab.

c) Click Tools.

d) Scroll down to "Weight and Spine calculator" and click.

e) Provide the requested information. Here's some help:

- ISBN is optional. You can leave this blank.

- Interior Color and Paper – Choose Color, then Standard 70.

- Binding Type – Choose Paperback, then Perfect Bound.

- Laminate Type – Choose Gloss.

- Duplex Cover – Choose No.

f) When you've provided all the necessary information, click Calculate.

The spine width will be displayed. For a 32-page picture book from IngramSpark with the above attributes, the spine width is 0.087".

4. Setting the front cover size

You're going to incorporate the spine into the front cover size, rather than create it separately. There are many reasons for this.

For one, the spine width is so narrow that the POD companies do not allow you to put text on it (for the title and author name).

For another, your book will look better with the narrow spine being a continuation of the front cover.

The cover's size depends upon whether you are using IngramSpark or KDP. They're a bit different. Let's look at KDP first.

a) KDP

To determine the front cover size for KDP, use these formulas:

Width = spine width + trim width + 0.125"

Height = 0.125" + trim height + 0.125"

For example, for an 8 x 10 trim size, the width of the front cover for a 32-page book would be 0.075 + 8 + 0.125 = 8.200".

The height would be 0.125 + 10 + 0.125 = 10.250".

b) IngramSpark

To calculate the front cover size for IngramSpark, use these formulas:

Width = spine width + trim width + 0.125"

Height = 0.125" + trim height + 0.125"

For example, for an 8 x 10 trim size, the width of the front cover for a 32-page book would be 0.087 + 8 + 0.125 = 8.212".

The height would be 0.125 + 10 + 0.125 = 10.250".

Now go ahead and create a new design for your cover!

5. Placing an illustration on the front cover

As discussed in the previous chapter, there are two basic approaches to creating your cover:

a) The illustration runs to the edges of the cover.

b) The illustration fits within the margins of the cover.

First, you'll learn how to make the cover when the illustration runs to the edge.

a) Illustration runs to the edges of the cover

Let's look at two scenarios:

  i.   You're using a new illustration created especially for the cover.

  ii.   You're re-using an interior illustration for the cover.

The workflow is a bit different for these, so it works best to handle them separately.

i.   New illustration

  1. Open Canva.

  2. Create a new design with the custom dimensions you arrived at in Section "4." above, "Setting the front cover size."

The new, blank design will appear in a new browser window, with the dimensions shown in the browser tab.

3. Give the new design a name that has the dimensions and "front cover" in it, and KDP or IS (for KDP or IngramSpark), so you know which POD company your design is for.

4. Since your illustrator has created a new illustration especially for the cover, upload it now. Then click on it to place it on your front cover. It will appear on the cover, but smaller than its original size.

5. To fit the illustration to the front cover, begin by pressing the Ctrl, Alt, and "f" keys at the same time. It won't be perfect yet. So the next step is to hold down the Shift key and stretch a side till the illustration is lined up with all the edges of your cover. Then zoom to 100% so you can check that its actual size is correct.

Now you're ready to create text for your title and contributor names, so go to Section "8" in this Chapter (page 107).

ii.   <u>Re-using an interior illustration</u>

1. Open Canva.

2. Go through your interior designs (p. 1-10, 11-20, 21-32) to find an illustration that best represents your story.

3. When you find the right illustration, click on it. Then copy it by pressing the Ctrl and "c" keys at the same time.

4. Return to your first Canva browser window (the one with your designs in the bottom half of the window).

5. Create a new design with the custom dimensions you arrived at in Section "4." above, "Setting the front cover size."

The new, blank design will appear in a new browser window, with the dimensions shown in the browser tab.

6. Give the new design a name that has the dimensions and "front cover" in it, and KDP or IS (for KDP or IngramSpark), so you know which POD company your design is for.

7. Paste the illustration you selected by pressing the Ctrl and "v" keys at the same time. It will appear on the cover, in its original size.

8. To fit the illustration to the front cover, start by pressing the Ctrl, Alt, and "f" keys at the same time. It won't be perfect yet. So hold down the Shift key and stretch a side till the illustration is lined up with all the edges of your cover. Then zoom to 100% so you can check and be sure.

Now you're ready to create text for your title and contributor names, so see Section "8" in this Chapter (page 107).

b) Illustration fits within the margins of the cover

Whether you're using a new illustration created especially for the cover or re-using an interior illustration, there's an important step you must take, *before* placing the illustration on the cover.

And that step is putting a "shape" on your design page that fills the page. Later, you will place your illustration on top of this shape.

Without this necessary step, you won't be able to assemble your front and back covers into one, super-wide cover for submission to your POD company.

i.   Placing a "shape" on your cover

a) Open Canva.

b) Create a new design with custom dimensions you obtained in Section "4." above, "Setting the front cover size."

The new, blank design will appear in a new browser window with the dimensions shown in the browser tab.

c) Give the new design a name that has the dimensions and "front cover" in it, and KDP or IS (for KDP or IngramSpark) so you know which POD company your design is for.

d) Now, on the left side of your screen, click "Elements," then "Shapes":

e) Click the first free square on the top left:

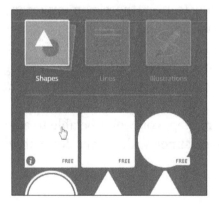

f) A black square will appear on your previously blank design. As the first step toward completely filling your design with the black shape, press the Ctrl and Alt and "f" keys at the same time. It won't be perfect yet. To make it perfect, hold the Shift key down while you stretch the shape. Zoom to 100% to make sure the black shape lines up with the edges of your design. Now it's perfect! See?

Now it's time to place your illustration on top of the black shape. (You'll change the color from black to something else later.)

We'll look at two scenarios:

ii.   You're using a new illustration created especially for the cover.

iii.   You're re-using an interior illustration for the cover.

The workflow is a bit different for each, so we'll handle them separately.

ii. New illustration

1. Since your illustrator has created a new illustration especially for the cover, upload it now. Then click on it, to place it on your front cover. It will appear on the cover, smaller than its original size.

2. Since you know the original width and height in inches of your illustrations, you can now convert inches to pixels. Just follow these steps:

   a) Go to www.unitconversion.org. In the search box, enter **pixel**.

   b) You'll get three options. Choose option "3. Typography: pixel (Y)."

   c) Choose "inch" in the "From" list. Choose "pixel (Y)" in the "To" list.

   d) Enter the width of your illustrations in inches. The width in pixels will appear. Make a note of this information. Then do the same for the height of your illustrations.

3. Now, go back to Canva, where you've placed your image on a design page.

4. To resize the image, use the double-headed arrow to drag the lower-right corner of the image until the numbers at the corner show the correct width and height in pixels. Bingo! That's the right size.

5. Click to end the resizing function.

6. Center the illustration on the page.

7. Change the color of the background shape from black to something else using ColorZilla. (See Section "2. Getting and Using ColorZilla.")

If you want to crop your illustration, refer to Section "6." If you wish to add a border to a cropped illustration, see Section "7."

If you want to do neither, then you're ready to create text, so see Section "8."

iii. <u>Re-using an interior illustration</u>

You're in good company here. The covers of *The Napping House* and *The Paper Bag Princess* re-use an interior illustration for the cover. To do this for your book, too, follow these steps:

1. Go through your interior designs (p. 1-10, 11-20, 21-32) to find an illustration that best represents your story.

2. When you find the right illustration, click on it. Then copy it by pressing the Ctrl and "c" keys at the same time.

3. Now go back to your cover design with the black shape on it.

4. Paste the illustration you selected by pressing the Ctrl and "v" keys at the same time. It will appear on the cover, in its original size.

5. Optional: You may want to shrink the illustration, to make room for the title and contributor names above and/or below it. That's what the cover of *The Paper Bag Princess* does in the edition I have. If you want to do this, too, simply resize by dragging a corner.

6. Center the illustration.

NOTE: If you did the optional Step "5." above, just center the illustration horizontally. Its vertical placement will depend on how much room you need for the title and contributor names.

7. Change the color of the background shape from black to another color using ColorZilla (see Section "2. Getting and Using ColorZilla").

If you want to crop your illustration, please see Section "6." If you wish to put a border around a cropped illustration, see Section "7."

If you don't need to do either, you're ready to create text, so see Section "8."

6. Cropping an illustration

For the cover of *The Napping House,* an interior illustration is cropped, and re-used for the cover. If you want to use this technique, too, follow these steps:

a) Before you crop an illustration, make a copy of your design to prevent you from cropping the original.

   To do this, first close the browser window that has the design you're working on. Then go to the Canva homepage that has all your designs in the lower part of the window. Refresh the browser. Scroll down to find the design you want.

b) Hover your cursor over the upper-right corner of the design until you see an arrow. Click the arrow:

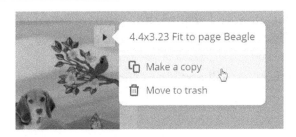

c) Click "Make a copy." Your copy will appear at the top of your collection of designs.

d) Click the copy. It will appear in a new browser window.

e) Click "Crop":

f) A cropping feature will appear on your illustration:

g) Adjust the location and size of the cropping area until you are satisfied. Then click the checkmark above the workspace.

h) Your cropped image will appear. (I've already centered it.):

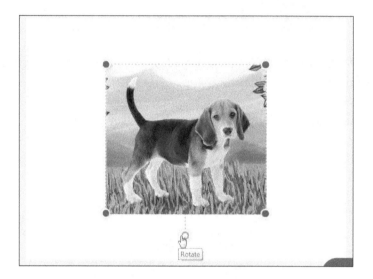

i) You may wish to enlarge the cropped illustration for use on your cover. Just drag a corner to resize.

You've just finished cropping (and possibly resizing) your illustration.

7. Putting a border around a cropped illustration

Putting a border around a cropped illustration is entirely optional, but I'm showing how to do it just to give you another option.

a) Click Search and then type **border**:

b) Scroll down and click the rectangular border with the solid line:

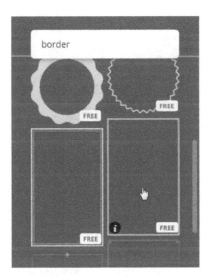

c) The rectangular border will appear over your cropped illustration:

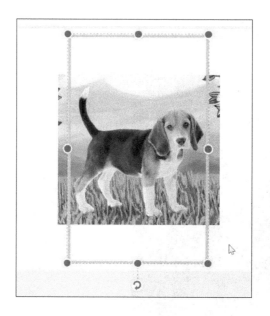

d) Resize the border to fit your cropped illustration:

Now you can change the color of the border with ColorZilla (see Section "2" in this Chapter).

8. Creating text

You already have a lot of experience creating text for your book's interior. This section will examine four points unique to the cover:

a) Creating multiple lines of text in different sizes.

b) Spacing out letters of a font to make it easier to read.

c) Using a shape as a background to the title.

d) Lining up contributor names to be on the same level.

Before we begin, I would like to point out that you don't always *have* to center your title on the cover. You could make it off-center if elements within the illustration come up high on one side (such as a tree trunk).

a) Multiple lines of text in different sizes

I showed you these two examples of titles in the previous chapter, and said that if your title is set on more than one line, make the less important text smaller, like this:

PIGS
ON A
RAFT

or this:

The
Trouble
with
Teddy

To use this style, follow these steps:

i.   Create each line of text separately, in its own size font and text box.

ii.   Select all the lines by holding down the Shift key while clicking each line.

iii.   Click "Group." After you do, your title will look something like this:

iv.   Click "Align," then "Align Horizontal Center":

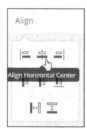

v.   You can see that the lines of text are now centered horizontally relative to each other:

vi.   Now click "Align" again. Then click "Vertical Distribute":

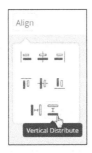

vii.   Now your text will be evenly spaced from top to bottom:

viii.   If you want to move the title to another place on the cover, keep the lines together as a group and move the group.

TIP: If you resize the text later, remember to re-align.

b) Spacing out letters of a font

The fonts **LUCKIEST GUY** and *Snickles* are very tight and crowded. And you may find other tight fonts you want to use. You can space the letters out and make them easier to read by following these steps:

    i.   Add text to your design page:

    ii.   Widen the text box so you have room to expand the space between the letters:

    iii.   Click "More":

    iv.   After you click "More," a menu will drop down. At the top of the menu, click "Text Spacing":

v.   After you click "Text Spacing," the following window will pop up:

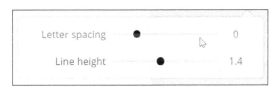

vi.   Click the "Letter spacing" button.

vii. Press the right-arrow key three times. Then click the "Letter spacing" button again. The zero (0) will turn to 30:

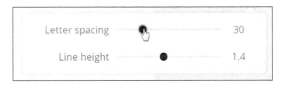

viii. Your text will be expanded:

You're done!

c) Using a shape as a background to the title

Sometimes, a title just won't stand out and be easy to read when placed directly over an illustration. When this happens, you can easily solve the problem by placing a solid shape under the title, like this:

To create a similar feature for your title, follow these steps:

i.   Open your front cover design.

ii. Click Elements, then Shapes:

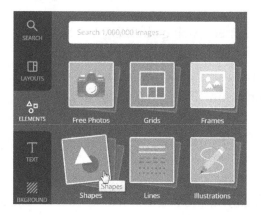

iii. Scroll way, way down, until you get to solid, colored shapes like these:

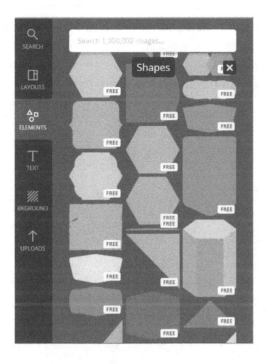

iv.   To select one, click on it.

v.   The shape will appear, centered over your cover. Move it up.

vi.   Adjust the size by dragging a re-sizing point.

vii.   Change the color if you want.

viii.   Place text over the shape.

ix.   Center the text over the shape.

Done!

d) Lining up contributor names

You'll only need this sub-section if you put the author's name on the left side of your cover, and the illustrator's name on the right.

Create them separately; then you'll line them up to be on the same level.

Here's what my cover looks like after I've placed the names at the bottom of the page. They're not lined up closely enough:

Now follow these steps:

    i.   To remove the ribbon of icons and tasks above your cover, click the workspace outside your cover:

ii. Now press the Ctrl and ; (semi-colon) keys at the same time. Then click above the top edge of your cover. The following icon will appear:

See it? The icon has arrows pointing up, and down, with lines between them.

iii. Click the icon; a horizontal dotted line will appear.

iv. Drag the icon and horizontal dotted line to the bottom of your cover, where the names are. (See below.) If, at any time, you move the illustration by mistake, just click your "best friend," **Undo**, and try again.

v. Now zoom to 100%:

vi. The names and horizontal dotted line will look like this:

vii. If you look closely, you can see that the author name is higher than the artist name. This is easy to fix. Just press the down-arrow key until the author name is lined up with the horizontal line:

Everything really begins to come together now!

viii.   To remove the horizontal dotted line, click the Ctrl and ; keys again at the same time.

And now you're done!

9. Ensuring front cover elements fit within the "safety zone"

Your front cover elements (such as text, and illustrations that don't run to the edge of the page), must all fit within a safety zone so they won't be trimmed during processing.

To do this, you'll create a small black box and line it up with the edge of the cover. Then you'll make sure your cover elements don't overlap the box.

The sizes of the boxes are different for IngramSpark and KDP on the bind side. Let's look at KDP first.

a) KDP

The small black box for the outside edges should be 0.625" wide by 0.625" high.

For the bind side, use this formula to determine the size of the box:

spine width + 0.5" = width of box for bind side

118

In our example, the spine width is 0.0751, so the size of the box for the bind side is 0.575" wide by 0.575" high.

b) IngramSpark

The small black box for the outside edges should be 0.625" wide by 0.625" high.

For the bind side, use this formula to determine the size of the box:

spine width + 0.5"= width of box for bind side

In our example, the spine width is 0.087, so the size of the box for the bind side is 0.587" wide by 0.587" high.

c) Creating and using small black boxes

To create small black boxes, follow these steps:

i.   Go to the Canva homepage which has all your designs in the lower part of the screen.

ii. Click "Use custom dimensions":

iii. The feature below will pop up. Change units to inches, and enter 0.625 for both width and height. (This box will check your outside edges.) Then click "Design!"

NOTE: Later, you'll make another box to check the bind side. You already have determined the correct size in Section "9.a" or "9.b" above.

After you click "Design!" your blank design will be displayed.

iv.   On the left side of your screen, click "Elements," then "Shapes":

v.   Click the first free square on the top left:

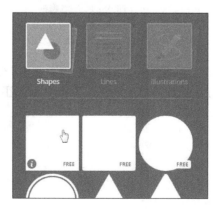

vi.   A black square will appear on your previously blank design. To make the square completely fill your design, press the Ctrl and Alt and "f" keys at the same time:

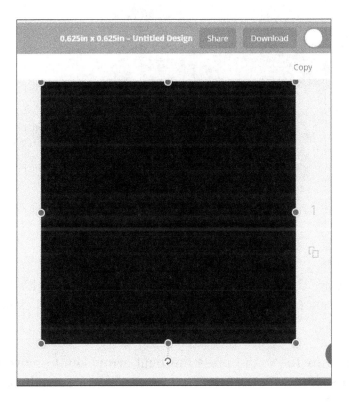

g)   Click the black shape and copy it by pressing the Ctrl and "c" keys at the same time.

h)   Go back to the browser window that displays your front cover design.

i)   Paste the black shape by pressing the Ctrl and "v" keys at the same time. Your design will look something like this:

xi.   Because the black shape has resizing circles on it, it's hard to see the actual size of the box. To remove the circles, click outside the box.

xii.   Zoom to 100% and press the right-arrow key to move the black box so it's above the title. Your cover will look something like this:

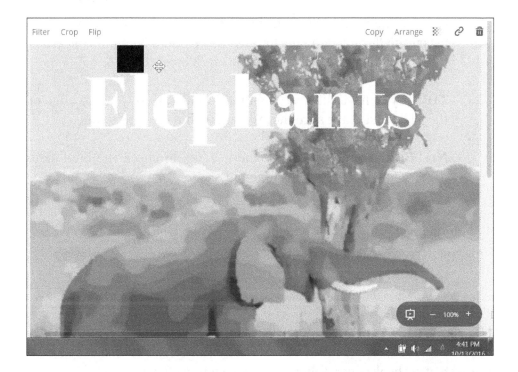

Notice that my title just fits under the black box. The title is in the safety zone. Great!

xiii.   Now move the black box down to the author's name to make sure it fits within the safety zone. If necessary, move the author's name, too. Your cover will look something like this:

In this example, the author's name fits just above the black box and is in the safety zone. The title and the author's name don't have to line up exactly with the black box. There can be space between the design elements and the black box. The main concern is that the elements don't overlap the black box.

TIP: If you have illustrations that do *not* run to the very edge of the page, just make sure they remain within the safety zone.

NOTE: Remember to make another box to check the bind side, the size of which you determined in Section "9.a" or "9.b" above.

xiv.   To remove the black box, click on it, then press the Delete key.

Now you're ready to create your back cover.

10. Creating your back cover

To create your back cover, follow the same steps as for the front cover.

However, there are three important considerations:

- Leaving room for the barcode

- The size of the little black box to check the safety zone for your design elements and

- The size of your back cover.

Let's tackle the size of your back cover first.

a) Setting the back cover size

The size of the back cover is the same whether you are using IngramSpark or KDP.

To determine the back cover size, use these formulas:

Width = 0.125" + trim width

Height = 0.125" + trim height + 0.125"

Example: For an 8 x 10 trim size, the width of the back cover for a 32-page book would be 0.125 + 8 = 8.125".

The height works out to 0.125 + 10 + 0.125 = 10.250".

b) <u>Setting the size of the little black box</u>

The sizes of the boxes are the same for IngramSpark and KDP.

The little black box for the outside edges of the back cover should be 0.625" wide by 0.625" high.

For the bind side, the box should be 0.5" wide by 0.5" high.

c) <u>Leaving room for the barcode</u>

You need to leave room on the back cover for the barcode, which your POD company will put on for you.

If you do not indicate where you want the barcode to go, your POD company will place it in its traditional location, the lower-right part of your back cover.

However, if you are using IngramSpark, the barcode really can go anywhere on the back cover, as long as you indicate to IngramSpark where you want it. Do this by placing a white rectangular box, the size of the barcode, on the back cover.

For IngramSpark, it's 1.75" wide x 1" high.

Ensure that the barcode area on your back cover is at least 0.5" from the edges of the back cover. Use your little black box for this.

To indicate where the barcode goes, follow these steps:

i.   Make a new design with the correct dimensions for the barcode.

ii.   Place a square shape on the new design by clicking Elements, then Shapes, and then the first free square shape.

iii.   Begin fitting the shape to the barcode design by pressing the Ctrl, Alt and f keys at the same time. Then hold down the Shift key as you stretch the shape until it fills the barcode design.

iv.   Click the black barcode shape. Then copy it by pressing the Ctrl and "c" keys at the same time.

v.   Go to your back cover and paste the barcode shape on it by pressing the Ctrl and "v" keys at the same time.

vi.   Change the color of the barcode shape from black to white. (Because the barcode itself needs a white background.)

vii.   Move the barcode shape to the desired location (an example is shown below). Make adjustments to your illustration or text if necessary so you have enough space for the barcode.

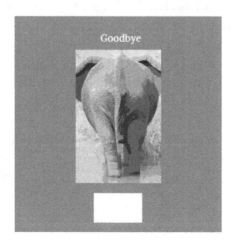

viii. Use a little box, 0.5" square, to make sure the barcode is at least 0.5" away from the edges.

ix. When you are satisfied, delete the 0.5" square box.

Congratulations! You've finished your back cover.

Now you will learn how to assemble your back and front covers into one super-wide cover that you'll submit to your POD company.

11. Assembling your cover

You've completed your front and back covers. Now you'll create a super-wide design, on which you'll paste them.

Your front cover will go on the right side of the super-wide design. Your back cover will go on the left.

a) Setting the size of the super-wide design

To find the proper total width of the super-wide design, simply add the width of your front cover to the width of your back cover.

The height of the super-wide design is the same as the height of your covers.

To create your super-wide design, follow these steps:

i. Go to the Canva homepage (the one with all your designs in the lower part of the screen).

ii. Click "Use custom dimensions."

iii. In the feature that pops up, change units to inches, then enter the width and height of your super-wide design. Click "Design!"

The color of the design will be white. Do *not* fill the design with a black shape.

b) Copying and pasting your front cover

Now it's time to copy your front cover and paste it on your super-wide design. Follow these steps:

    i.   Go to your front cover. Click on the background shape, or the illustration, that runs to the edges of the front cover. The black circles that appear on each corner and side of the cover mark the edges:

    ii.   Copy the background shape or the illustration by pressing the Ctrl and "c" keys at the same time.

    iii.   Go to your super-wide design and paste the background shape or illustration by pressing the Ctrl and "v" keys at the same time.

    iv.   The background shape or illustration will appear on the left side of your super-wide design. Move it to the right by pressing the right-arrow key. Make sure the right edge lines up with the right edge of the super-wide design. Zoom to 100% to check. (Always a good idea!)

v. Return to your front cover design. De-select the background shape or illustration that runs to the edges by clicking anywhere outside your design. The black circles will disappear from each corner and side of the cover.

vi. To select the other elements of your cover, such as an illustration on top of a background shape and/or text, hold down the Shift key while clicking each element.

You do *not* want the selected elements in a "Group." If they are in a group, "Ungroup" will appear. Click it:

vii. Copy the selected elements by pressing the Ctrl and "c" keys at the same time.

viii. Return to your super-wide design. Paste the selected elements by pressing the Ctrl and "v" keys at the same time.

ix.   The selected elements will appear on the left side of your super-wide design. Move the selected elements to the right by pressing the right-arrow key:

c) Copying and pasting your back cover

Now you'll copy your back cover and paste it on your super-wide design. (The steps are similar to those for the front cover.) Follow these steps for the back cover:

i.   Go to your back cover. Click on the background shape, or the illustration, that runs to the edges of the back cover. You can tell you've selected it by the black circles which appear on each corner and side of the cover.

ii.   Copy the background shape or the illustration by pressing the Ctrl and "c" keys at the same time.

iii.   Return to your super-wide design. Paste the background shape or illustration by pressing the Ctrl and "v" keys at the same time.

iv.   The background shape or illustration will appear on the left side of your super-wide design—exactly where it's supposed to be.

v. Return to your back cover design. De-select the background shape or illustration that runs to the edges by clicking anywhere outside your design. The black circles will disappear from each corner and side of the cover.

vi. To select the other elements of your cover, such as an illustration on top of a background shape and/or text, hold down the Shift key while clicking on each element.

You do *not* want the selected elements in a "Group." If they are in a group, "Ungroup" will appear. Click it.

vii. Copy the selected elements by pressing the Ctrl and "c" keys at the same time.

viii. Go back to your super-wide design. Paste the selected elements by pressing the Ctrl and "v" keys at the same time.

ix. The selected elements will appear on the left side of your super-wide design. And that's exactly where they should be!

x. Zoom to 100% to check that the front and back covers align with the outside edges. Also, make sure the front and back covers ad-join each other near the center of the super-wide design, with no space between them:

xi.   Zoom out to view your completed super-wide cover:

Your super-wide cover is done! You're getting even closer to your finished product.

Later, you'll learn how to download the cover in the format your POD company needs.

For now, let's do the last bit of work for your book's interior: the title page.

12. Creating your title page

Since you now have a lot of experience creating covers and interior pages, in this section I won't give you step-by-step help. I will, however, provide you with useful guidelines.

The easiest way to make your title page is to copy elements you want to re-use from your cover and paste them onto your title page.

Ideally, you would use an illustration for your title page that is different from your front cover.

Remember that your title page is the same size as the rest of the pages inside your book. Therefore, if the interior illustrations for your story fit within a 0.5" margin, you must keep this margin for the title page illustration, too.

In any event, don't let the *text* on your title page extend past the margins you've set for the rest of the pages inside your book.

NOTE: If your book's interior is the same size as the trim size, the background color of the title page can only be white.

13. Getting feedback

I have given you guidelines and suggestions in this chapter, but feedback on your covers from your critique group or other people whose opinion you trust can only improve your finished product—and even boost your confidence. If possible, show them different versions to see which they like best.

Now's a good time to consult with a professional graphic designer. While friends can tell you whether they like a cover or not, they usually can't give specific suggestions for improving it.

A professional graphic designer can offer tried-and-true concrete advice, such as changing the background color, or the color or size of text, to optimize your finished product.

Below is a list of skilled professional graphic designers with specific experience designing children's picture book covers. Since they wouldn't be doing actual design work, but only giving feedback, the cost for a consult is modest, but their expertise is valuable.

Tell them I sent you, since, in some cases, I have negotiated a special price for my readers.

Each accepts payment via PayPal.

Here they are, in alphabetical order:

Alyssa Cooper, Ontario, Canada
Alyssa@AlyssaCooperArts.com
www.AlyssaCooperArts.com

Cost for feedback on cover: $25 for a one-paragraph critique.

Alyssa writes, "Feedback will include comments on font choice and readability, as well as textual hierarchy, general layout and composition, quality/relevance/originality of cover photos and/or illustrations, color scheme, and overall impact. The feedback will be specific to the book's genre, as each genre has its own dos and don'ts when it comes to what works in a cover."

I asked Alyssa what "textual hierarchy" means, and she answered, "Textual hierarchy refers to which text on the cover draws the eye most quickly - for example, a writer with a large following will want their own name more prominent, whereas a lesser known author will want to make the title more prominent, and writers of series may want the series title to draw more attention than the individual title, etc."

I also asked Alyssa if she meant sub-genres within the overall genre of children's picture books, and she answered, "And yes, I did mean sub-genres within the main genre of kids' books - there are different age brackets to consider, as covers for very young children are treated differently than those for school-age/middle-grade children, as well as different formats (narrative, ABC, educational, etc.), and different subject matter. Purchasing decisions are often made based on the cover exclusively, so if your cover treatment doesn't accurately reflect the age/style/content of your book, you'll be missing out on readers or misleading customers, which can lead to poor reviews."

Luciana Guerra, Buenos Aires, Argentina
LiquidMindArt@gmail.com
www.LiquidMindArt.com

Cost for feedback on cover: $15

Luciana writes, "The feedback includes: advice and comments about the fonts, composition, colors and images and the guidance needed until the cover is totally finished."

Noura Pemberton, Houston, Texas, USA
nouraguru@gmail.com
www.nouraguru.com
www.guru.com/freelancers/noura

$25 per hour; Noura says a written critique will take one hour.
Office Hours 6AM - 11AM Houston, Texas Time (Monday - Friday)

Noura writes:
"As part of the initial feedback, I will focus on the following areas:
1. Marketability aspects of the book cover
2. Relativeness to the subject
3. Eye-catching aspects
4. Improvement suggestions
5. What other similar best-selling books have for covers"

Csongor Veres, Budapest, Hungary
This is a man's name.
verescsongor@gmail.com
http://verescsongor.wixsite.com/childrenillustration

$20 per hour; Csongor says a one-page, written critique will take one hour. If you need more feedback than that, the cost would be an additional $20 (not per hour; just an additional $20) until the cover is done.

Csongor writes:
"This [book] is a very nice idea to help people to make their dreams come alive. I would be happy if my feedback can help these writers to improve their skills and experiences in cover design.

I can guide them from start to finish, including advice about the font style, the layout, how to play with fonts and how to make them as a part of the cover images. The back cover is very important to match together with the front cover, so I can help them with this also."

Send the graphic designer a "PDF-Standard" of your covers. To do this, follow these steps:

a) Go to Canva and click on your cover design.

b) Click the Download button.

c) On the small window that pops up, click the down arrow and choose "PDF-Standard." The PDF will be downloaded to your "Downloads" folder.

d) To open your "Downloads" folder, click the arrow next to the filename at the bottom-left of your computer screen, and choose "show in folder."

e) Your file will be highlighted. Rename the file so it has "Standard" in it.

f) Copy the file to the folder for your book files.

If the designer asks also to see the book's interior (to better evaluate the cover), send a "PDF-Standard" by following the above steps.

You've done great work here! Take a break now, and when you've rested up, we'll set up an account and title with your POD company.

The next chapter, Chapter 9, will lead your through setting up a KDP account.

The following one, Chapter 10, will show you how to create an IngramSpark account.

Chapter 9
Setting up an Account and Title
with KDP

This chapter explains how to contact Customer Support and how to set up an account and title. Have your credit or debit card handy, as well as your bank account and routing numbers.

At the end of this chapter, using Canva, remember to put your ISBN on your copyright page.

Customer Support

On the KDP Dashboard, click the "Help" link, then the "Contact Support" button.

You will be prompted to choose what your question is about, and then to choose "Issue Details." You can also select "Other."

The next screen will give you the choice to "Send us an email" or "Call us." The fastest way to get support is to have them call you back, so click the "Call us" option.

Enter your phone number and choose either "Call me now," or "Call me in 5 minutes." If you choose "Call me now," a customer support representative will call you back immediately, which is great!

The hours for telephone support are currently 6 AM to 5 PM Pacific Time, Monday through Friday.

Setting up an account

Use your browser to go to kdp.amazon.com.

If you've never used KDP before, you'll need to create an account. Click the "Sign up" button.

Then just follow the simple on-screen directions.

Setting up a new title

On your KDP Bookshelf, under "Create a New Title," click the "Paperback" button.

The next screen asks for basic title information, which is self-explanatory.

Formatting your book description

KDP allows formatting with basic HTML, a set of codes which allows you to format your description with bold, italic, underline, etc. for display on a browser.

Don't know HTML? No problem. Just go to Dave Chesson's Web page at kindlepreneur.com/html-generator. It's fabulous!

Dave's page lets you format your description with bold, italics, lists, etc. Then, with the click of a button, it gives you your description with the appropriate HTML codes. You'll find them below the box where you formatted your description.

Highlight the coded version and copy it by pressing the Ctrl and "c" keys at the same time. Then paste it into the book description area on KDP by pressing the Ctrl and "v" keys at the same time.

TIP: Don't get carried away adding bold, italics and underlined text! Just because you *can* use them, *doesn't* mean you must. Very often, "less is more." (But it sure is nice to know it's all available.)

Provide the relevant information this screen asks for, and then click "Save & Continue."

Selecting an ISBN option

The next step is selecting the correct option for your ISBN. If you ordered one or more ISBNs directly from the ISBN agency, choose to give your own ISBN. Otherwise, just choose the option for a free KDP-assigned ISBN.

If you chose to give your own ISBN, a space will open where you can enter your own ISBN and imprint name.

If you chose the option for a free, KDP-assigned ISBN, you will now see your assigned ISBN. **Write down the ISBN for future reference.**

Click "Save as Draft" at the bottom of the page. This will save your work. You'll complete the rest later, when you're ready to upload your book files. When you get to that stage, I'll guide you through it. For now, just close your browser.

Putting your ISBN on your copyright page

Go to Canva and type your ISBN on your copyright page.

You've set up your account and title. In Chapter 11, you'll learn how to download your Canva designs and prepare your book files.

Chapter 10
Setting up an Account and Title
with IngramSpark

This chapter explains how to contact Customer Support, and how to set up an account and title. Have your credit or debit card handy, as well as your bank account and routing numbers.

At the end of this chapter, using Canva, remember to put your ISBN on your copyright page.

Customer Support

There are three ways to contact IngramSpark customer support: email, online chat, and phone.

Phone

The phone number for IngramSpark customer service is 1-855-997-7275. The hours are 7 AM to 7 PM Central Time, Monday through Friday; and 10 AM to 7 PM Saturday and Sunday.

They may answer "Lightning Source." Don't let that confuse you because Lightning Source is the parent company of IngramSpark. You've come to the right place. The customer service representatives are the same people for both divisions.

Be prepared to give your IngramSpark account number, which is located on the top-right corner of any IngramSpark page once you've logged in.

Online chat

After you log in to your account, online chat is available. Just click the Support button in the lower-right corner of any IngramSpark page. Be prepared to provide your account number.

Email

Their email address is ingramsparksupport@ingramcontent.com. If you use this option, put your account number in the Subject. It will probably take a couple of days for them to reply.

This is the slowest method of customer support.

Setting up an account

Before you sign up for IngramSpark, go to Google and search for **IngramSpark coupon code**. You may find a coupon button for a free title setup. If you do, click on the Coupon button, which will take you directly to IngramSpark to sign up. Your discount will be applied when you set up your title.

If you find only a code for a discount (and not a clickable button), write down the code so you can use it later. Then go to www.IngramSpark.com and click the Start Publishing button to sign up.

When you sign up for IngramSpark, you will be asked for some information about yourself. Here are two fields you might need help with:

Business or Legal Name – If you have a business, enter its name. If you don't, enter your own name.

Form of Business – If you don't have a company, choose Sole Proprietor.

After you submit your information, IngramSpark will send you an email with a link to activate your account. Click on the link to go to an IngramSpark page.

Use the Login link at the top of the IngramSpark page. After logging in and agreeing to general terms of the site, you will be taken through four agreements. You are required to digitally sign the first two (by typing your name), but it doesn't mean you're required to use those services. It just means that you have those services on your account if you choose to use them later. Here are the agreements:

1. Global POD (required) – You'll use this agreement to distribute your printed children's picture book. It's for Print-on-Demand (POD) services via Lightning Source companies in the US, UK, Australia. This agreement also applies to the Global Connect and Espresso POD networks (an automated POD book-making kiosk).

2. Global Ebook (required) – Although you must agree to this, you probably won't use it since almost all ebook sales come from Amazon. This agreement is for ebook distribution services to IngamSpark's Distribution Partners *except* for Amazon Kindle and Apple.

   If you decide to use this agreement, you'll have to pay $85 for an ISBN! It's not worth it! (The ISBN for your ebook is paid for once and applies to Agreements 2, 3 and 4.)

3. Amazon (Kindle) Ebook (optional) – You should opt out because this book explains how to create an ebook for free in the format Amazon Kindle uses and then how to upload it directly to Amazon.com.

   Working with Amazon.com directly means that your ebook will be available faster, and you can make changes faster (to the description and price, for example), than going through IngramSpark.

   And, if you were to go through IngramSpark to sell your ebook on Amazon.com, you would have to pay $85 for an ISBN, while going directly to Amazon.com means you get a unique identifier (called an ASIN) for free.

Be aware that if you uploaded an ebook directly to Amazon in the past 12 months, you may *not* sign this agreement with IngramSpark.

4. Apple (Agency) Ebook (optional) – This agreement is for distributing your ebooks to Apple's US and International iBooks and iTunes stores. Since almost all ebook sales are through Amazon Kindle, you don't really need this agreement. However, if you decide to use it, you'll have to pay $85 for an ISBN (as explained above).

You'll still have a few tasks left to do before your account is fully active, including giving IngramSpark information for paying you. Most of this is very straight-forward. Simply follow the directions on the IngramSpark Dashboard.

However, there are two bits of information you may need help with. One is about claiming a tax exemption. You *do* want to claim a tax exemption, and when you're asked how you qualify, choose "Claiming exemption based on resale."

The other bit of information you may need help with is your "Title" for tax purposes. If you used your Social Security Number, you can just enter "Writer" for your Title.

Note that IngramSpark will pay you 90 days after the end of each month in which sales were made.

Setting up a new title

On your IngramSpark Dashboard, click the "Add a New Title" button.

Set up *only* the Print version of your book with IngramSpark (and *not* the ebook, as explained earlier).

You will be asked for your book description. This is very important because customers will read it to decide whether to buy your book. Get feedback on your description from your critique group or others whose opinion you value. But don't worry; you can always add or edit it later by going to the IngramSpark Dashboard and clicking the title of your book.

As you set up your title and have a question about a specific field, click the "?" for help. There's plenty of it.

You may need additional help with the following information requested on the Print Format screen:

- ISBN – You can get this when you set up a new title with IngramSpark. They give you a discount; currently, an ISBN costs $85. **Write down the ISBN for future reference.**

- Interior Color and Paper – Choose Color, then Standard 70.

- Binding Type – Choose Paperback, then Perfect Bound.

- Laminate Type – Choose Gloss.

- Duplex Cover – Choose No.

When you get to the screen that asks what discount you want to give, you have basically two choices. If you want to make your book available to bookstores, enter 55%.

If you've decided to forego bookstore sales, and want to sell your book only through online retailers (like Amazon.com), enter 30%. This is the smallest discount IngramSpark allows and will enable you to maximize your earnings on each copy sold on Amazon.com and other online retailers. (This is significantly more than you can make with KDP.)

Another bit of information you may need help with is the On Sale Date. This is the date you release your book for printing. If you set it to the current date, you can order a copy of your book (to check for mistakes) before you put it into distribution.

For "Returnable?" choose Yes if you're selling to bookstores. Choose No if you're selling to online retailers.

You can set up your title without uploading your book files immediately. When you get to the "Title Files" page, simply click Cancel. When your book files are ready, you can go back to upload them. You'll learn how to do this when we get to that stage.

Putting your ISBN on your copyright page

Go to Canva and type your ISBN on your copyright page.

Now that you've set up your account and title, you're ready to download your Canva designs and prepare your book files.

Chapter 11

Downloading Canva Designs and Preparing Book Files

This chapter shows you how to download your four finished Canva designs—three for the interior of your book and one for the cover.

Then, you'll combine the interior files into one PDF.

If you plan to submit your files to IngramSpark, I'll also show you how to rename the final PDF files according to IngramSpark's standards.

This chapter covers:

1. downloading finished Canva designs as PDFs

2. combining PDFs

3. renaming files for IngramSpark.

Before starting, make sure you've put your ISBN on your copyright page.

1, Downloading finished Canva designs

You'll do files one at a time.

a) Open Canva.

b) Open a finished design.

c) Click the Download button.

d) You'll see that the default is "PNG (Recommended)." Ignore that. Click the down arrow. A drop-down menu will appear. Scroll down to "PDF-Print" and click.

e) The finished design will be saved in your "Downloads" folder.

f) Copy the file to a folder you've created for your book files.

Repeat these steps for each finished design.

2, Combining PDFs

By now, you have three "PDF-Print" files for the interior of your book. Here's how to combine them into one PDF.

a) Go to www.freepdfsolutions.com/pdfmerge.html. Download and install the free, easy-to-use program.

   NOTE: To download, scroll to the very *bottom* of the page and click on the *reddish-brown* DOWNLOAD button. Don't be tempted to click any other buttons on that page, as they will take you to other software that doesn't have the functionality you need.

   NOTE: Please don't use a free online PDF-combining program. I've tried them all! They either can't handle the file sizes or they bloat the combined file size, making it considerably larger than desirable. Even more frustrating is that the combined file won't successfully upload to IngramSpark.

b) Open PDFMerge by double-clicking the icon on your desktop. A window will appear:

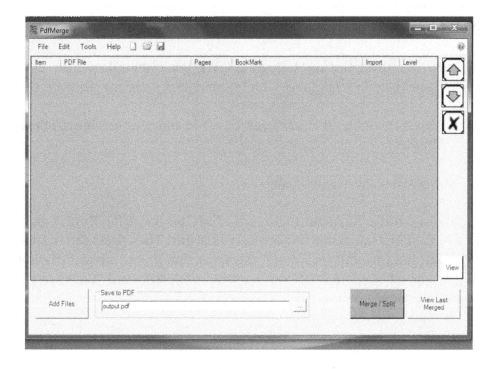

c) Click the "Add Files" button each time you want to add an interior PDF file. Add your files in the order they should appear in your final book.

d) After you add all three PDF files, click the "Merge/Split" button.

e) Your PDFs will be combined and saved in the correct folder with the filename "output.pdf." (Go look.)

f) Open your combined PDF (output.pdf) and confirm that it has all your pages in the correct order.

If you're submitting your files to KDP, you're finished and can upload the cover and interior PDFs with the filenames they already have.

3, Renaming files for IngramSpark

If you're submitting the files to IngramSpark, you can't upload them until you rename them in accordance with IngramSpark's naming guidelines.

a) Open the folder that has your cover file and your combined interior file.

Now you'll make a copy of each file.

b) To do this, highlight the interior file ("output.pdf"). Do not highlight *just* the name. Include the whole line. Then press Ctrl+c (that is, the Ctrl and "c" keys at the same time). Next press Ctrl+v. A copy of the interior file will appear, with the word "Copy" in the file name.

c) Repeat "b" for your cover file.

Now you'll rename the "Copy" files so they're acceptable to IngramSpark.

d) For your interior file, name it **ISBN-txt**.

e) For your cover file, name it **ISBN-cvr**.

Congratulations! You're now ready to submit your files to IngramSpark.

The next chapters will show you how to submit your book files to KDP or IngramSpark.

Chapter 12
Submitting Your Book Files
to KDP

You now have two PDFs: one for the interior of your book and one for the cover. You are now ready to submit them both to KDP.

Submitting your PDFs

Go to your KDP Bookshelf and click the "Continue setup" button next to the title of your book. This will take you to the "Paperback Details" page. When you are satisfied with everything you've entered, click the "Save and Continue" button.

The next page is for "Paperback Content."

Under "Print Options," choose "Color interior with white paper."

Then choose your Trim Size, or enter your own.

Another part of the screen asks you about the "Bleed." If the pictures inside your book are smaller than the trim size, choose "No Bleed." If your book's pictures run to the very edge of the page when the bleed is trimmed, choose "Bleed."

For the finish of your cover, choose Glossy.

Now, you're ready to upload the PDF for the interior of your book. Click "Upload paperback manuscript."

An area will open for you to browse your computer and choose your interior file.

For the "Book Cover," click the button next to "Upload a cover you already have." Then browse for your cover file and upload it.

Once your uploads are complete, click the "Launch Previewer" button. An automated print check will run, and you can see your book's interior and cover online using the Previewer tool.

At the bottom of the page, you'll see a summary of your book details, and the printing cost.

When you are satisfied with the layout, click "Save and Continue" to set up your distribution and pricing, and to order a proof.

Proofs

IMPORTANT: You've checked out the e-proof version online, but you absolutely *must* order a printed proof (a copy of the book) *before you publish!*

After you order a proof, click the "Save Draft" button on the "Paperback Rights & Pricing" page.

Within four hours of ordering a proof, Amazon will send you an email with a link for completing your purchase of the proof.

Examine the printed version carefully to ensure there are no mistakes or other things you'd like to change.

NOTE: The colors in your printed book will not look the same as on your computer monitor because they use entirely different color systems.

Submitting revisions

If there is something in your book's interior or cover you'd like to change, go to your KDP Bookshelf and click the ellipsis menu ("...") associated with the title of your book. Choose "Edit Paperback Content."

Then follow the online instructions for uploading the PDF for the interior and/or cover.

When you submit a new PDF to KDP, the new file will overwrite the old one.

There is no charge for revisions.

Approve proof and enable distribution

When you are satisfied with the printed copy, go back to your Bookshelf and click on the ellipsis ("...") menu associated with the title of your book. Click "Edit Paperback Rights & Pricing."

Scroll down the page until you see the button "Publish Your Paperback Book." Take a deep breath and click it.

In my experience, it takes from 12 to 24 hours for a KDP book to appear on Amazon.

Your book is now available to the world!

A note about Kindle

Immediately after you've published your print book with KDP, you will be given the option to publish it as an ebook with Kindle.

Since their automated conversion process does not know how to handle children's picture books, just say, "No, thanks."

When they ask you why not, choose, "I'll do it later."

Congratulations! You've published your children's picture book. Take pride in knowing it's an actual, professional-quality, printed book.

Now what do you do? If you want to publish an ebook on Amazon.com, see Chapter 14. If you don't, go directly to Chapter 15, "After You Publish."

Chapter 13
Submitting Your Book Files
to IngramSpark

You now have two PDFs: one for the interior of your book, and one for the cover. Finally, they're both ready to submit to IngramSpark.

Submitting your PDFs

Go to your IngramSpark Dashboard and click the title of your book. This will take you to the set-up pages.

Step through the pages until you get to the last page, which is for uploading your PDFs for the interior and cover.

After uploading them, you will be asked to approve the submission. Once you do, you'll receive a confirmation.

Approve the e-proof

It should take two to three days for IngramSpark to process your files and prepare an e-proof.

When the e-proof is ready for your review, the Status column on your Dashboard will reflect this. You'll also receive an email.

If there are no mistakes on IngramSpark's part, you can approve the e-proof, but ***don't*** put your book into distribution yet.

Before you do that, order a printed copy.

Check the printed copy

Check the printed version carefully. Make sure there are no mistakes or other things you'd like to change.

NOTE: Always remember that the colors in your book will not look the same as those on your computer monitor because they use entirely different color systems.

Submitting revisions

If there is something in your book's interior or cover you'd like to change, go to your IngramSpark Dashboard and click the title of your book. This will take you to the Details page.

At the top of the Details page is a button for uploading new files. Click it. Follow the online instructions for uploading the PDF for the interior and/or cover.

When you submit the new PDF to IngramSpark, the new file will over-write the old one.

You will be charged $25 for each new PDF.

Enable distribution

When you are satisfied with the printed copy, return to your Dashboard and click the title of your book. This will take you to the Details page.

Scroll down the page until you see the "Enable" distribution button. Take a deep breath and click it.

In my experience, it takes about a week for a book to appear on Amazon.

Congratulations! You've published your children's picture book. Take pride in knowing you've created an actual, professional-quality, printed book.

And better yet: **Your book is now available to the world!**

Now what do you do? If you want to publish an ebook on Amazon.com, the next chapter will show you how. If not, go directly to Chapter 15, "After You Publish."

Chapter 14

How to Make an eBook for Free
to Sell on Amazon.com

This is your bonus chapter! Here, I'll show you how to make an ebook for free to sell on Amazon.com.

One advantage of setting up your ebook directly with Amazon.com is that you don't need to pay for an ISBN. Amazon.com will assign a unique identifier for free.

If you were to go through IngramSpark to sell your ebook to Amazon.com or anywhere else, you would have to pay $85 for an ISBN. And it's definitely not worth it!

However, working with Amazon.com directly means that your ebook will be available faster and you can make changes more quickly (to the description and price, for example), than going through IngramSpark.

This chapter covers the following:

1. Using Canva to download your front cover as a "JPEG"

2. Using Canva to download "Standard" PDFs of your book's interior and your front cover

3. Using PDFMerge to create a single "Standard" PDF for Kindle Kids' Book Creator

4. Getting Kindle Kids' Book Creator

5. Creating a folder for your ebook

6. Creating an ebook using Kindle Kids' Book Creator

7. Previewing your ebook

8. Formatting your ebook description for Amazon.com

9. Creating a KDP account

10. Uploading your ebook and cover to Amazon.com.

Let's begin!

1. Using Canva to download your front cover as a "JPEG"

Amazon needs your front cover file to be in the JPEG format (pronounced JAY-peg) to put on your ebook's Product page. To prepare a JPEG, follow these steps:

a) Go to Canva and click on your front cover design, the first one you created.

b) Click the Download button.

c) On the small window that pops up, click the down arrow and choose "JPEG." The JPEG of your front cover will be downloaded to your "Downloads" folder.

d) To open your "Downloads" folder, click the arrow next to the file-name at the bottom-left of your computer screen, and choose "show in folder."

e) Your file will be highlighted. Rename the file so it has "Kindle" in it.

f) Copy the file to the folder for your book files.

Now you have a JPEG of your front cover to submit to Amazon.

2. Using Canva to download "Standard" PDFs of your book's interior and front cover

Work on each file one at a time for accuracy and efficiency.

a) Go to Canva and open the first design for your book's interior, starting with pages 1-10.

b) Click the Download button.

c) Click the down arrow; a drop-down menu will appear. Scroll down to "PDF-Standard" and click.

d) The finished design will be downloaded to your "Downloads" folder.

e) To open your "Downloads" folder, click the arrow next to the file-name at the bottom-left of your computer screen, and choose "show in folder."

f) Your file will be highlighted. Rename the file so it has "Kindle" in it.

g) Copy the file to a folder you've created for your book files.

Repeat these steps for each part of your book's interior, *and for your front cover design*, the same one you made a JPEG of.

NOTE: You will not be downloading your back cover because you don't need one for an ebook.

3. Using PDFMerge to create a single "Standard" PDF for Kindle Kids' Book Creator

You've already used PDFMerge to combine PDFs for your POD company. You'll use it again for Kindle. Follow these steps because they're a little bit different this time:

a) Open PDFMerge by double-clicking the icon on your desktop. A window will appear:

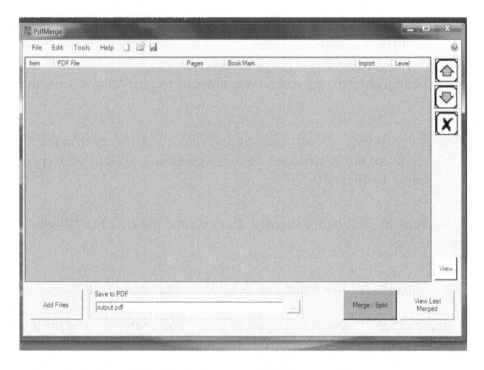

b) Click the "Add Files" button each time you want to add a PDF file. Start with the PDF of your front cover. Then add the PDFs of your book's interior, in the order you want them to appear in your final ebook.

c) When you add all four PDF files, look for "Save to PDF" at the bottom of the window, and change the filename from "output.pdf" to **"output-Kindle.pdf."**

d) Click the "Merge/Split" button.

e) Your PDFs will be combined and saved in the correct folder, with the filename "output-Kindle.pdf." (Go ahead and look!)

f) Open your combined PDF (output-Kindle.pdf) and confirm that it has your front cover and all your interior pages, in the correct order.

Now that you have your PDF for Kindle, you'll get Kindle Kids' Book Creator.

4. Getting Kindle Kids' Book Creator

Kindle Kids' Book Creator is the program you'll use to create an ebook for Amazon. To get it, follow these steps:

a) Use your browser to go to kdp.amazon.com.

b) Click KDP Kids.

c) Click Get Started.

d) Under "Prepare Illustrated Books," click "Download for PC."

e) Install the program on your computer.

5. Creating a folder for your ebook

Before you use Kindle Kids' Book Creator, create a new, empty folder in which you will save your Kindle ebook.

6. Creating an ebook using Kindle Kids' Book Creator

The first time you use Kindle Kids' Book Creator, double-click the icon on your desktop. On the window that pops up, click "Create a New Kids' Book...."

a) The window that pops up has an explanation, but you don't need it if you follow the steps here. Click Continue.

b) On the next window, provide details about your book, including the title, the author and language. Also indicate where on your computer you want to save your Kindle book. Select the new folder you just created. Then click Continue.

c) On the next window, Page Orientation, choose Portrait if your book is taller than it is wide. (This is most common.)

   Choose Landscape if your book is wider than it is tall; then choose "One image at a time," so your text won't be too small to read.

d) On the next window, opt to import your entire book, including the cover, from a PDF (the default). Click the button "Create Book from PDF" and select the "output-Kindle.pdf" file you created in this chapter for the Kindle.

e) From the File menu, select "Save for Publishing...."

f) A window will appear, with the file name already entered, and the extension as .mobi (for Kindle ebooks). Click Save.

Your ebook will be created for you.

The next section will show you how your ebook will look on various reading devices.

7. Previewing your ebook

In Kindle Kids' Book Creator, go to the Book Preview menu item and select "Create Book Preview...." The Book Preview will be created for you.

To see the cover, select "Go to," then Cover.

Click the tabs for the different Kindle devices to see how your ebook will look on each device.

If there is anything you want to change about your book information, click the tab for Book Settings and select Metadata. Make any necessary changes and click "Save for Publishing..." again.

When you are satisfied, you're ready to format your ebook description for Amazon.com.

8. Formatting your ebook description

You should have already written your book description because your POD company asked for it when you set up a title with them. You can, and should, use the same description for your ebook, *with the addition of this sentence*: "This ebook is a print replica."

If you set up your printed book title with KDP, you can re-use the HTML-coded description, with the addition of the "print replica" sentence.

If you set up your printed book title with IngramSpark, keep reading this section.

Amazon's Kindle Direct Publishing allows formatting with basic HTML, a set of codes that allows you to format your description with bold, italic, underline, etc. for display on a browser.

Don't know HTML? No problem. Just go to Dave Chesson's Web page at kindlepreneur.com/html-generator. It's fabulous!

Dave's page lets you format your description with bold, italics, lists, etc. Then, with the click of a button, it gives you your description with the appropriate HTML codes. You'll find them below the box where you formatted your description.

TIP: Don't get carried away adding bold, italics and underlined text! Just because you *can* use them, *doesn't* mean you must.

When you set up your Amazon Kindle ebook title, you can copy your HTML-coded book description and paste it in the description area that Amazon provides.

Now let's create a KDP (Kindle Direct Publishing) account.

9. Creating a KDP account

Before you upload your ebook and cover to Amazon.com, you'll need to create a KDP (Kindle Direct Publishing) account (if you don't have one already), and add a new title. Simply follow these steps:

a) Use your browser to go to kdp.amazon.com.

b) If this is the first time you're visiting KDP, follow the instructions to create a new account.

10. Adding a New eBook Title

a) On your Dashboard, under "Create a New Title," click on "Kindle eBook" and enter the required ebook details (title, author name, illustrator name, etc.).

b) For the Description, copy and paste the one you formatted with HTML codes.

c) To proceed to the next step, click "Save and Continue."

11. Uploading your ebook and cover to KDP

A very straight-forward procedure, Amazon lets you browse your computer files to upload your ebook and cover.

To upload your ebook, choose the Content file from your Kindle book folder.

To upload your cover, select the JPEG version of your front cover.

When Amazon notifies you that your files have been successfully uploaded, click "Launch Previewer." Check the online proof. If there any changes you wish to make, you can upload new files now.

You'll notice that an ISBN is optional. You don't need one to publish an ebook on Amazon.com. They will assign a unique identifying number (called an ASIN) to your ebook for free.

To proceed to the next step, click "Save and Continue."

12. Pricing

a) Regarding KDP Select, choose No. By signing up for KDP Select, you agree to offer your ebook for free to customers who have a Kindle Unlimited subscription.

Instead of a retail price, you get paid for each page they read, based on a given month's KDP Select Fund (which is often $20 Million). But don't get too excited because the bottom line is that with KDP Select, you'll wind up making only a few pennies on a given month's sales. Better to earn a regular royalty, which amounts to far more.

b) Select the territories you have the rights to sell your title in (probably worldwide).

c) I suggest that you set your Retail Price between $0.99 and $2.99 so your ebook will be competitive. (You can always change it later.)

d) Choose the royalty you want (probably 70% in the eligible countries).

REMEMBER: You can change any of the above information later by going to your Dashboard and selecting Edit Details for your ebook.

e) When you are satisfied, click "Publish Your Kindle eBook."

That's it! Amazon informs you that it may take up to 48 hours for your book to appear on Amazon.com, but, in my experience, it usually only takes a couple of hours.

Chapter 15
After You Publish

This short chapter discusses what to do after you've published your book.

Register your copyright

Go to www.copyright.gov to register your copyright. You need to be online, and your computer must be connected to a printer.

Just register yourself, as the author. Let the illustrator handle her own copyright.

It costs about $35 to register.

You'll need to know the Publication Date. If you don't remember it and you published your book through IngramSpark, go to your IngramSpark Dashboard, click the title, and check the Details page for the Publication Date.

If you published through KDP, you can find the Publication Date immediately on your Dashboard.

Order two copies of your book to send to the Copyright Office. Do that ASAP because you have only 30 days from the time you register your book online until they receive it.

While you're registering online, print out two copies of the Packing Slip, one for each copy of your book. Attach a Packing Slip to each copy, and mail both copies together in one envelope to the Copyright Office.

As of this printing, it has been taking about nine months to receive your copyright certificate.

Register your book with MyIdentifiers

MyIdentifiers (www.myidentifiers.com) is a Website owned by the ISBN agency. Use it to register your book if you purchased your own ISBN. This way, your book will appear in Books in Print, and be available to book buyers.

Be ready to provide details about your book, and to upload a JPEG file of the book cover. (See Chapter 14, Section "1" for how to create a JPEG.)

Promote your book

The subject of promotion would fill an entire book. I highly recommend you start with the following:

- *How to Market a Book* by Joanna Penn

- *How to Get Great Book Reviews Frugally and Ethically* by Carolyn Howard-Johnson

- *www.Kindlepreneur.com* by Dave Chesson

- *www.BookReviewTargeter.com* by Debbie Drum.

If you've followed the suggestions and "how-to" help in this book, you've created a professional-quality children's picture book, one you can be proud to promote. Creating a high-quality product that you believe in will make all your efforts worthwhile.

Good luck!

Afterword

Thank you for taking this journey with me. I've enjoyed being your guide.

If you have any questions, please email me at:

EveHeidiWrites@gmail.com

I will answer your questions and address your concerns, and use them to improve this book for its next edition.

I wish you much success!

Kind regards,

Eve Heidi Bine-Stock
Author of the three-volume series,
How to Write a Children's Picture Book

Website: www.EveHeidiWrites.com

CPSIA information can be obtained
at www.ICGtesting.com
Printed in the USA
BVHW050509040121
596837BV00010B/680